to Pearl

the Kingdom first!

HOWARD WOLGEMUTH
1537 N.W. Parkgate Dr.
Kissimmee, Florida 32741

Disciple

Disciple

by Juan Carlos Ortiz

Creation House
Carol Stream, Illinois

ISBN 0-88419-101-X
Library of Congress Catalog Card Number 74-29650

FOREWORD

Juan Carlos Ortiz. What a man and what a writer! The following pages will introduce you to one of God's most beautiful and humble servants in Latin America today. Juan Carlos Ortiz is real; he pulls no punches. He writes like he talks and talks like he writes. And what he writes is not stuffy theory based on a few things he has taken from dusty books in a Buenos Aires library. On the contrary. His message of encouragement to the Church is central in the wide-ranging set of experiences of a concerned pastor in the Argentine capital.

The illustrations Juan Carlos uses will make you think. They will also make you cry. If you are like me, some of the stories he shares will double you up with laughter. There is a little bit of everything in these pages. So here's fair warning: Once you get into this book I guarantee you will be hooked. You may not want to sign your name to all of Juan Carlos' theology or to his various interpretations. But don't let that stop you. Keep reading, because whatever disagreement you may have will soon become unimportant as he shares freely and honestly what God is accomplishing through His people in Latin America today.

The theme is love: brother love, neighbor love, mashed potato love, and other varieties. Juan Carlos then quickly reminds us that for the follower of Jesus this love must work itself out in a radical, no-nonsensical understanding of Christian discipleship. To Juan Carlos, the equipping and training of individual men and women for service is what the Church is all about. And this book is definitely about the Church.

Juan Carlos is my dear brother and friend. I am personally delighted that his clear, uncluttered message is no longer restricted to our neighbors in Latin America, because here is a man of God who is saying things that the Church around the world needs to hear today.

When you have finished these pages you just may want to give Juan Carlos a big, warm Latin *abrazo* (a hug); and regardless of the quality of your Spanish accent you will certainly want to say, *muchas gracias*.

Dr. W. Stanley Mooneyham
President
World Vision International

CONTENTS

PART ONE

THE NEW WINE

What is a disciple? A disciple is one who follows Jesus Christ. But because we are Christians does not necessarily mean we are His disciples, even though we are members of His Kingdom. Following Christ means acknowledging Him as Lord; it means serving Him as a slave. It also means loving and praising.

That is what the first part of this book is about.

1

The "Gospel According to the Saint Evangelicals"

"And why do you call Me, 'Lord, Lord,' and do not do what I say?"

—*Luke 6:46*

We have an interesting problem in Spanish with the word *lord*. *Lord* is *señor,* the same word we use for *mister*. We say Señor Smith, Señor Williams, and Señor Jesus. It's as if in English you were to say Mr. Smith, Mr. Williams, and Mr. Jesus.

The result in Spanish is that we have lost the "lord" concept. To call Jesus the Lord *(Señor)* doesn't really say anything very strongly.

But since I have come among English-speaking people, I have found that you have the same problem, even though you have two separate words, *mister* and *lord,* in your language. Maybe it is because you think of the lords of England, who

11

sometimes haven't been so admirable.

Lord doesn't mean today what it meant when Jesus was here. Back then it meant the maximum authority, the first one, the one above everything else, the owner of all creation. The Greek word *kurios* ("lord") in small letters was how slaves addressed their masters. But if the word was capitalized, it referred to only one person in the whole Roman Empire. Caesar of Rome was *the Lord*. As a matter of fact, when public employees and soldiers met in the street, they had to say as a greeting, "Caesar is the Lord!" And the standard response was, "Yes, the Lord is Caesar!"

So the Christians had a problem. When they were greeted with "Caesar is the Lord!" they answered, "No, Jesus Christ is the Lord." That immediately got them in trouble. Not because Caesar was jealous of the name. It was far deeper than that. Caesar knew that the Christians really meant that they were committed to another authority and that in the balance scale of their lives, Jesus Christ weighed much more than Caesar.

They were saying, "Caesar, you can count on us for some things, but when forced to choose, we will stay with Jesus, because we have committed our lives to Him. He is the first one. He is the Lord, the maximum authority over us." No wonder Caesar persecuted the Christians.

The gospel which we have in the Bible is the gospel of the Kingdom of God. It presents Jesus as King, as Lord, as the maximum authority. Jesus is at the very center. The gospel of the Kingdom is a Christ-centered gospel.

But in recent centuries we have been hearing another gospel—a man-centered, human gospel. It is the gospel of the big offer. The gospel of the hot sale. The gospel of the irresistible special deal. The minister says, "People, if you will accept Jesus—" (You see, there is already a problem, because it is Jesus who accepts us, not vice versa. But we have put man in the place of Jesus, so man is very important now.)

The evangelists say, "Poor Jesus is knocking at the door of your heart. *Please* open the door. Don't you see Him standing out there in the cold in the snow? Poor Jesus—open the door for Him." No wonder the listener thinks he would be doing Jesus a great favor to become a Christian.

We have told people, "If you accept Jesus, you will have joy, you will have peace, health, prosperity . . . . If you give Jesus ten dollars, you will get twenty dollars back . . . ." We are always appealing to man's interests. Jesus is the Savior, the Healer, and the King coming for *me*. *Me* is the center of our gospel.

Our meetings are man-centered. Even the arrangement of the furniture, the chairs, the pulpit points to man. When the pastor makes out his order of service, he doesn't think about God but rather about his audience. "For the first song everyone will stand—for the second they will be seated because they will be tired—then we will have a duet just to change the atmosphere a little—then we will do something else—and it all must fit into one hour so the people don't get too tired." Where is Jesus, the Lord?

Our hymns are the same way. "Count your blessings"—"Jesus belongs to me"—"I am satisfied with Jesus." Our prayers are man-centered. "Lord, bless my home, bless my husband, bless my cat, bless my dog, for Jesus' sake, amen." That prayer is not for Jesus' sake at all—it's for *our* sake! We often use the right words, but we use them with the wrong attitude. We fool ourselves.

Our gospel is like Aladdin's lamp; we think we can shake it and receive everything we like. No wonder Karl Marx called religion the opiate of the masses. Perhaps he was right; he was not a fool. He knew that our gospel is often an escape for people.

But Jesus Christ is not an opiate. He is the Lord. You must come and give yourself to Jesus and fulfill His demands when He speaks as Lord.

If our leaders had been threatened by the police and the high priest as the apostles were, they would probably have prayed, "O Father, be merciful to us. Help us, Lord. Be mer-

13

ciful to Peter and John. Don't let the soldiers touch them. Please give us a way of escape. Don't let us suffer. Look at what they are doing to us. O Lord, stop them and don't let them do us any harm." Us, we, I, me.

But when we read Acts 4, the praying was just the opposite. Notice how many times the apostles said *Thou* and *Thy*.

> They lifted their voices to God with one accord and said, "O Lord, it is Thou who didst make the heaven and the earth and the sea, and all that is in them,
> who by the Holy Spirit, through the mouth of our father David Thy servant, didst say,
> 'Why did the Gentiles rage,
> And the peoples devise futile things?
> 'The kings of the earth took their stand,
> And the rulers were gathered together,
> Against the Lord, and against His Christ.'
> "For truly in this city there were gathered together against Thy holy Servant Jesus, whom Thou didst anoint, both Herod and Pontius Pilate, along with the Gentiles and the peoples of Israel,
> to do whatever Thy hand and Thy purpose predestined to occur.
> "And now, Lord, take note of their threats, and grant that Thy bond-servants may speak Thy word with all confidence,
> while Thou dost extend Thy hand to heal, and signs and wonders take place through the name of Thy holy Servant Jesus."
> And when they had prayed, the place where they had gathered together was shaken, and they were all filled with the Holy Spirit.

No wonder! It couldn't be any other way after their God-centered praying.

I am not just talking about semantics; I am talking about the tremendous attitude problem we have in the churches. It's not enough that we change our vocabularies; we must let God take out our brains, wash them in detergent, brush them, and put them back in the other way. Our whole set of values must be changed.

We are like the medieval people who thought the earth

was the center of the universe. They were wrong, and so are we. We think we are the center of the universe, and God and Jesus Christ and the angels all revolve around us. Heaven is for us; everything is for our benefit.

We are wrong. God is the center. We must change our center of gravity. He is the sun, and we revolve around Him.

But it is very hard to change. Even our motivation for evangelism is man-centered. I remember hearing many times in Bible school, "Oh, students, look at the lost souls. They are perishing. The poor people are going to hell. Each time the clock strikes, another 5,822½ persons go to hell. Are you not sorry for them?" And we wept. We said, "Poor people! Let's go and save them." You see, we went not for Jesus' sake, but for lost souls' sake.

That may look nice, but it's wrong, because everything must be Christ-motivated. We do not preach to lost souls because they are lost. We go to extend the Kingdom of God because God says so, and *He is the Lord.*

Our modern gospel is what I call the Fifth Gospel. We have the Gospel according to Saint Matthew, the Gospel according to Saint Mark, the Gospel according to Saint Luke, the Gospel according to Saint John, and the Gospel according to the Saint Evangelicals. The Gospel according to the Saint Evangelicals is taken from verses here and there in the other four Gospels. We take all the verses we like, all the verses that offer something or promise something—John 3:16, John 5:24, and so forth—and we make a systematic theology from these verses, while we forget the other verses that present the demands of Jesus Christ.

Who authorized that? Who said we are allowed to present only one side of Jesus? Suppose there is a wedding, and when it's time for the vows, the man says, "Pastor, I accept this woman as my personal cook." Or "as my personal dishwasher." What?

The woman would say, "Wait a minute! Yes, I'm going to cook. Yes, I'm going to wash dishes. Yes, I'm going to clean the house. But I'm not a maid—I'm going to be your wife. You have to give me your love, your heart, your home, your talent—everything."

The same is true with Jesus. He is our Savior and our Healer, true. But we cannot cut Jesus Christ into pieces and take only the piece we like best. We are like children who are given bread with jam; they eat the jam and hand back the bread. You put on more jam, and they again eat the jam and give you back the bread.

The Lord Jesus is the Bread of Life, and maybe heaven is like the jam. We have to eat the bread as well as the jam.

Wouldn't it be interesting if some big congress of theologians would decide that there is no heaven or hell? How many people would stay in their churches after that announcement? Most of them would quit. "If there's no heaven or hell, why are we coming here?" They have come only for the jam, for their own interests—to get healed, to escape hell, to get into heaven. They are following the Fifth Gospel.

When Peter finished his sermon on the Day of Pentecost, he made it clear: "Therefore let all the house of Israel know for certain that God has made Him both Lord and Christ—this Jesus whom you crucified" (Acts 2:36). That was his theme.

When people realized that Jesus was actually the Lord, they were "pierced to the heart" (verse 37) and began to tremble. "Brethren, what shall we do?" they asked.

The answer: "Repent, and let each of you be baptized in the name of Jesus Christ for the forgiveness of your sins; and you shall receive the gift of the Holy Spirit" (verse 38).

Paul's gospel was summarized in Romans 10:9: "That if you confess with your mouth Jesus as Lord, and believe in your heart that God raised Him from the dead, you shall be saved." He is the Lord. He is much more than Savior.

I will give an example of this Fifth Gospel. Luke 12:32 says, "Do not be afraid, little flock, for your Father has chosen gladly to give you the kingdom." Ah, this is a popular verse, I've preached many times from this text.

But what about the next verse? "Sell your possessions and give to charity." I've never heard a sermon on this verse, because it is not in the Gospel according to the Saint Evangelicals. Verse 32 is part of our Fifth Gospel, but verse 33 is not—and it is a command from Jesus.

Jesus commanded us not to kill.

Jesus commanded us to love our neighbor.

Jesus commanded us to sell our possessions and give to charity.

Who has the right to decide which commandments are compulsory and which are optional? You see, the Fifth Gospel has made a strange thing: an optional commandment! You do it if you want; if you don't, that's all right, too.

But that's not the gospel of the Kingdom.

2

The Gospel of the Kingdom

*"Come unto me, all who are weary and heavy laden, and I
will give you rest."*
"Take My yoke upon you, and learn from Me . . . ."
                        —Matthew 11:28-29

We like to hear about the first verse, verse 28. But Jesus'
words, "Take My yoke upon you," are not so popular.

Salvation is not only freedom from your burdens and
problems. Yes, you get free of that yoke, but you get another
one to replace it—Jesus' yoke. He frees you from all your old
burdens in order to use you for His Kingdom. He delivers you
from your problems that you may have His problems. You
now live for the King, not for yourself.

I could perhaps say that the Fifth Gospel is composed of
all the verses we have underlined. If you want to read the
gospel of the Kingdom, go back and read the verses you *never*
underlined, because that is the truth you lack. I do not

underline the Bible anymore, because underlining divides the verses into first class and second class. I used to underline my Bible in many colors, but now I leave everything in the same color. Everything is important.

In the Old Testament, Jesus was always presented as the coming Lord and King. He is greater than Moses, David, or the angels. Even David called him "my Lord" (Psalm 110:1).

How did Jesus introduce Himself to Zaccheus? If instead of Jesus, one of us twentieth-century pastors would have been trying to contact him, we'd have said, "Are you Mr. Zaccheus? It's nice to meet you."

"Oh, uh, nice to meet you, I'm very pleased."

"Mr. Zaccheus, I would like to have a few words with you, sir. Could you possibly look at your calendar—I know you're a very busy man—but maybe I could have an appointment. Is there a time when it would be convenient?"

That would leave Zaccheus with a choice. He would say, "Well, is it important?"

"Well, I think it's very important, although you might not agree."

"Well, let's see, this week is all full. Maybe next week sometime."

Jesus never did anything like that. He looked up into the tree and gave an order: "Zaccheus, hurry and come down, for today I must stay at your house." When you are the Lord, you don't give people a choice. Salvation is not a choice; it is a command.

Zaccheus now had to decide what to do with the command. He had to obey or disobey. (No wonder Jesus said once, "He who is not with Me is against Me." He polarized people one way or the other.) To obey means acknowledging that Jesus is the authority, the Lord. If Zaccheus disobeyed, he would become Jesus' enemy.

He decided to obey. He swung down out of the tree and led Jesus and the apostles to his house. As soon as he got inside the door, he said, "Honey, please fix some food for these people."

His wife probably said, "Darling, why didn't you tell me you had invited guests for lunch?"

"Honey, I didn't invite them—they invited themselves!" Jesus doesn't need any invitation. He is the Lord of all houses and all people.

After awhile, Jesus said, "Today salvation has come to this house." When was Zaccheus saved? No one had explained the plan of salvation. No one had spelled out the Four Spiritual Laws. When was Zaccheus saved? When he *obeyed* the Lord. The minute he came down out of that tree, he placed himself under the lordship of Jesus Christ.

The same thing happened with Matthew. He was collecting taxes. Jesus didn't stand beside him waiting until a free moment when he could say, "Hello, hello, I'm Jesus. It's awfully nice to meet you. I know you're very busy—oh, here wait . . . ." No. That would have given Matthew the choice of whether to pay attention to Jesus or not. Jesus said, "Matthew, follow Me!" It was not an invitation. It was a command. Matthew had to obey or disobey. This is the gospel of the Kingdom: "Repent, and believe!" You either will or you won't.

The same thing happened to the rich young ruler. He asked, "Good Teacher, what shall I do to obtain eternal life?" (Luke 18:18). He had done almost everything.

Jesus said, "One thing you still lack; sell all that you possess . . . and come, follow Me" (verse 22).

The young man went home very sad.

What would we have done? We would have run after him and said, "Young man, don't take it so seriously—come along just the same. We will make a special arrangement . . . ."

That would have meant he could follow Jesus, but on his own terms.

Jesus, even though He loved him, let him go. Had Jesus lowered His requirements, the young man would never have truly been saved from himself.

Jesus commanded another man to follow Him once, and the man said, "Permit me *first* to go and bury my father" (Luke 9:59).

We would have said, "Of course, of course—forgive me for calling you just now. Oh, poor fellow, I'm so sorry. You take two or three days for the burial."

No! Jesus said to let others take care of the burial; He was much more important than a dead father or anyone else. The man had agreed to follow Jesus, but "permit me first . . . ." Who is first but Jesus? Here was another who wanted to follow Jesus on his own terms. And Jesus said, "No, it's on My terms."

Jesus obviously could have let him go bury his father. But there was a principle involved.

Another man said, "I will follow You, Lord; but first permit me to say good-bye to those at home" (Luke 9:61).

Jesus could have said, "Of course. Go and have a dinner with your family, and tell them thanks for letting their son come with Me." But Jesus never gave that choice.

We are not saved because we agree to a certain doctrine or formula. We are saved because we obey what God says. All Jesus says is, "Follow Me!" He doesn't say where, or how much He will pay us. He just gives the command.

Salvation is a commandment. God wants everyone to be saved, because all have sinned. So He commands us to repent. If we don't, we are disobedient to God. This is why there is a punishment for people who don't repent. If it were only an invitation, there would be no punishment.

Suppose you say to me, "Juan Carlos, would you like to have a piece of cake?"

And I say, "Oh, no, thank you."

And then you begin punching me with your fists.

"Why are you whipping me?"

"You didn't accept my cake."

"But you just invited me to have it—why should I be punished?"

Repentance is a commandment, not an invitation. Otherwise, Jesus shouldn't punish people who refuse.

If Jesus would have let the young ruler come along without selling His possessions, he would have been a spoiled disciple. Every time Jesus commanded him to do something, he would have said to himself, *Well, shall I do it or not?* That's the kind of people we have in our churches because we have been preaching the Fifth Gospel.

Salvation is submission. Salvation means coming under Christ. You may not understand what atonement or propitiation means, but you can understand what it means to submit to the Lord. You become a citizen of His kingdom. You are covered by His protection.

What does the Lord's Prayer mean when it says, "Thy kingdom come. Thy will be done, on earth as it is in heaven"? It means I must abdicate the throne of my life where I have been sitting and let Him sit on the throne. Before I met Jesus, I was the commander of my life. Since I met Him, He commands.

"Thy will be done on earth" is something for right here and now, not for tomorrow or the ages to come. We modern ministers have not only diluted the gospel of the Kingdom, we have set it up in comfortable monthly payments. It's like buying a car. With ten dollars you get the whole car, but then you keep on paying.

Maybe we're trying to sell the gospel like we sell cars. We say, "You want to be saved? Just raise your hand, that is all."

How is that all? That's the first payment. After a while, someone will say, "Do you know about baptism? We're going to have a baptismal service soon—it will be a nice warm spring day, and we'll heat the water, and a group is going to be baptized?" This is a second payment.

And if the person says, "Oh, no, I really don't care to," we say, "Fine, of course not, you can wait until you're ready."

This was not the message in the primitive church. They said, "Repent! Be baptized!" It was a command, not an option.

Then after a long while comes another payment: "You know, brother, we have to support all the things we're doing here in the church, and so we tithe our money. But it's not as bad as it sounds, because when you tithe, the ninety percent goes further than the 100 percent did before. God will stretch the money for you."

It's a man-centered gospel.

What happens is that we vaccinate people against the real gospel of the Kingdom with these little doses once in a while. Then we wonder why we preach and preach and preach and it doesn't seem to penetrate the people.

Jesus said, "Seek first His kingdom and His righteousness; and all these things shall be added to you" (Matthew 6:33). What things? The context is clear—food, clothing, shelter, the elementary things of life. People are often asking the Lord, "Please give me a better job." "Lord, give me this or that." If they have to ask for these things, then they must not have them. And the reason they don't have them is that they are not seeking first the Kingdom of God.

God promised all these things to people who seek His Kingdom. All I have to do is seek His Kingdom, and when I look around I will say, "Where did I get all these things? They must have been added to me while I was seeking His Kingdom."

If a person from another planet were to come and see how Christians live, he would think that Jesus had said something like this: "Seek ye first what you are going to eat, what you are going to wear, which house you are going to buy, which car you are going to drive, which job you are going to take, who you are going to marry—and then, if any time is left, and if it's not too uncomfortable, please do something for the Kingdom of God."

Once I asked a man, "Why do you work?"

"Well, I work because I have to eat. If I don't work, I don't eat."

"Well, why do you eat?" I asked.

"So I will have strength to work."

"And why do you work again?"

"Well, I work again to eat again to work to be able to eat . . . ."

That's not life. That's just breathing. There is no purpose to it.

Then one day I understood. My purpose is to extend the Kingdom. Jesus said, "All authority has been given to Me in heaven and on earth" (Matthew 28:18). He must conquer the whole universe for God. The Father has said to Him, "Son, I won't take care of My enemies. You will do that for Me. You will reign until all the enemies are under Your feet. Then we will talk again."

Jesus came to this earth and told His disciples, "I'm the commander-in-chief of the armies of God. I must conquer the universe for My Father. But to you I give the charge of this planet. You must go into all the world and make disciples everywhere, baptizing them and teaching them to obey all My commandments. Meanwhile, I'll go to conquer other worlds. Good-bye, and do a good job."

So inch by inch I must recover the things that belong to God. To do that, I have to eat; to eat, I have to work. But the purpose of it all is to extend the Kingdom of my Lord.

That means my values have to change. I don't study at the university to get a degree; I am there as a member of Christ's Kingdom to do Kingdom business. I also happen to get a degree.

I don't work at Ford Motor Company to earn my livelihood. I work there because God needs that spot on this earth; He needs one of His soldiers to conquer it for Him. And Mr. Ford happens to support my conquest. But my real Lord is Jesus Christ.

Or else I should stop using the name. Because Jesus asks, "Why do you call Me, 'Lord, Lord,' and do not do what I say?"

3

Servants of the Kingdom

"But which of you, having a slave plowing or tending sheep, will say to him when he has come in from the field, 'Come immediately and sit down to eat'?

"But will you not say to him, 'Prepare something for me to eat, and properly clothe yourself and serve me until I have eaten and drunk; and afterward you will eat and drink'?

"He does not thank the slave because he did the things which were commanded, does he?"

—Luke 17:7-9

We have discussed what a lord is. Now we shall see what a servant is.

Jesus was talking to people who knew the real meaning of the word *slave.* We don't have such persons today; the closest comparison is the servant or maid who works for wages, has a firm contract in advance, and belongs to a union.

But the servant in the first century was a genuine

slave—a person who had lost everything in this world. His liberty, his freedom, his will, even his name was gone. He had been sold in the market as an animal. A price had been hung around his neck, and people had bargained for him. Someone had eventually bought him, taken him home, and bored a hole in his ear so he could wear a ring with his master's name on it. He had thereby lost his name; he was no longer John or Peter, but the slave of Mr. Johnson or Mr. Brown.

He was paid nothing for his work. He had lost every freedom. If his owner said, "You must get up at six o'clock," he got up at six. If his owner said four o'clock, he got up at four. If his owner wanted something done at midnight, he had to do it. He was a slave. No freedom. No choice. Nothing.

So when Jesus told His little story about a master inviting his slave to eat first, the disciples laughed. No one would do that. The slave had to serve the master first—always. He had to wash up, change clothes, fix the meal, serve the meal, and then after the master had eaten and gone to bed, the slave could stay around and eat the leftovers.

When Jesus said, "He does not thank the slave because he did the things which were commanded, does he?" the people answered, "Of course not."

Jesus then concluded, "So you too, when you do all the things which are commanded you, say, 'We are unworthy slaves; we have done only that which we ought to have done' " (Luke 17:10).

We may not like to hear it, but it is true: We are the slaves of Jesus Christ. We were bought by the Lord. Paul understood this entirely when he wrote, "Not one of us lives for himself, and not one dies for himself; for if we live, we live for the Lord, or if we die, we die for the Lord; therefore whether we live or die, we are the Lord's. For to this end Christ died and lived again, that He might be Lord both of the dead and of the living" (Romans 14:7-9).

27

We've heard so often that *Jesus* died for *our* sins. That's only part of the story. The reason He died and was resurrected, says Paul, was to be the Lord of all us slaves. He explains it very wonderfully in 2 Corinthians 5:15—"He died for all, that they who live should no longer live for themselves, but for Him who died and rose again on their behalf."

So we have been bought with a price. That's why the New Testament says so often, "Paul, a bond-servant of Christ Jesus . . . ," "James, a bond-servant of God and of the Lord Jesus Christ . . . ," "Simon Peter, a bond-servant and apostle of Jesus Christ . . . ." Even Mary called herself "the bondslave of the Lord" (Luke 1:38).

We were lost before we were found by our owner. We were headed for eternal damnation.

But listen to another truth: We are still lost. We used to be lost in sin, in the hands of Satan. Now we are lost in the hands of Jesus.

Many people think salvation means to be made free. "Oh, praise the Lord—now I'm free, free, free!" Well, not quite. "Having been freed from sin, you became slaves of righteousness" (Romans 6:18).

You see, there are two masters in this world, and each has a kingdom. We were born into the kingdom of darkness. We were natural citizens of the kingdom of selfishness. It is a place where everyone does his own will. That is the way Satan runs his kingdom, "in the lusts of our flesh, indulging the desires of the flesh and of the mind" (Ephesians 2:3).

We lived as we liked. We did as we pleased. What difference did it make? The kingdom of darkness is like a wrecked ship that is sinking fast. When the captain knows his ship is lost, he goes to the passengers and says, "Listen, those in second class can go to first class; you're free to do what you want. Anyone who wants to drink, help yourself at the bar; it's all free. If you want to play soccer in the dining room, go ahead. If you break the lamps, don't worry."

The passengers say, "What a nice captain we have! We can do whatever we like on this ship."

But they will all be dead in a few minutes.

In the kingdom of darkness, you can have all the drugs, lust, and cheating you want. Nevertheless, you are lost. You think you are the king. You are led by the selfish spirit of your kingdom. But it is only a matter of time.

What is salvation? It is to be "delivered . . . from the domain of darkness, and transferred . . . to the kingdom of His beloved Son" (Colossians 1:13). It is not getting free of the kingdoms altogether. It is moving from the rulership of Satan to the rulership of Jesus Christ.

In this new Kingdom, you cannot do whatever you like. You are part of the Kingdom *of God*. He is the King. He rules. We live according to His wants and wishes.

Some people think the distinctives of God's Kingdom are that we don't smoke and drink and go to the movies. It is much deeper than that. In God's Kingdom, we do whatever God says. He is the Lord of the Kingdom.

The testimony of those who have passed from death to life, from one kingdom to the other, is this: "Before I met Jesus, I ran my own life. But since I met Him, He rules."

Some people wish it weren't so clear-cut. They live and think as if there are three ways, not two. The wide way is for sinners headed for hell. The narrow way is for the pastors and missionaries. And then there's a third way, not so wide, but not so narrow—a medium way for the rest of the believers. Of course, this is not in the book of doctrine. But it is in the book of reality where people live.

The medium way is an invention of man. Either we are in the kingdom of darkness doing our own will, or we are in God's Kingdom doing His will. There is no in-between.

In fact, it's fairly difficult to get from one kingdom to the other. There are no passports or visas. We are *slaves* of our own sin. We can't just walk off from it—no slave can do that. The only way to get free of slavery is to die. Why did the American slaves sing about heaven so much? It was their only hope of freedom. So we can only be free of sin by dying.

And there's another problem: The Kingdom of God does not accept naturalized citizens. You have to be born into the Kingdom. Suppose the laws of the United States were like that. And I came along to the immigration office and said, "I want to be an American."

"Where were you born?" they would ask me.

"Buenos Aires, Argentina."

"Then you cannot be an American," they would explain, "because all Americans are born on American soil."

"Oh, but sir, I really want to become an American."

"Where were you born?"

"Buenos Aires."

"Well, I just told you that the only way to be an American is to be born in the United States of America."

"Oh, sir, how can I do it? I really truly want to be an American."

"Well, the only thing you can do would be to die and be born again, and this time be sure to be born in America. That's the only way. We don't accept visitors. We don't accept visas anymore. You have to be born here."

So how can a man change citizenship from the kingdom of darkness to the Kingdom of God?

Jesus brought the solution. His death on the cross and His resurrection really means this· Any slave who looks to the cross in faith is allowed to count that death as his own death. He dies; Satan loses him.

Then comes the resurrection. By it we are transferred into the new Kingdom. This is just as important as the cross. We die to one king and are born under the rule of another.

This is what baptism is all about. For a long time, I was baptizing people, but it was just a ceremony for me. It was a nice ceremony—we had photographers, we had nice robes, we had a choir singing in the back; it was quite a show. That was before God started to renew us. Now we understand that baptism has a meaning. It should be done right away, as soon as the person begins to live in the new Kingdom. It doesn't matter to me so much whether it's by immersion or whatever—the Bible is not as plain on that as it is on, say, loving one another (and we don't do that!). But immersion does show in a very plain way His death and resurrection. We put the person down into the water, but we don't leave him there. We bring him up again.

This is not just our idea, or an idea of the apostles'. Baptism is done "in the name of the Father, and of the Son, and of the Holy Spirit." The person is actually baptized by God, with a man acting in His name.

In Argentina we sometimes use this baptismal formula: "I kill you in the name of the Father, and of the Son, and of the Holy Spirit, and I make you born into the Kingdom of God to serve Him and to please Him." It's different, but it works much better.

Some people think that salvation is through baptism alone; others say through faith alone. But the apostles said, "Repent and be baptized!" Both things. They didn't say, "He who believes and is saved will, after a few months, be baptized." They said that baptism has a meaning in salvation.

What is the meaning? It is like a dollar bill. The bill has two values. One is the intrinsic value, the value of the paper and ink—which isn't too much. One penny would buy a much larger piece of paper, and a little green ink would make many bills.

But there is a greater, different value to the dollar, because it is backed by the federal reserves of the United States of America. You take the green piece of paper to the supermarket and they give you many things (well, a few, anyway).

So it is with baptism. The water, the ceremony is not much. But the ceremony is backed by what Jesus Christ did on the cross and in the tomb. And so baptism has a tremendous value. It tells the person being baptized that he is passing from death to life. That's why it needs to happen at the moment of passing.

This is not something I have invented. The primitive church never baptized anyone after the first day they were converted. They didn't even wait for the evening meeting. If someone was saved in the morning, he was baptized in the morning. If he was saved in the middle of the night, as the Philippian jailor in Acts 16, he was baptized in the middle of the night.

So in Argentina we do not assure a person of salvation until he is baptized, not for the sake of baptism but for the sake of obedience. If a person says, "I believe," but doesn't want to go through with baptism, we doubt his committment to the new Kingdom. Because obedience is what salvation is all about.

If we are not close to a river or a pool, it's no problem—we go ahead and baptize the person in his own bathtub in his own house. We baptize the man, his wife, and his children all in the same tub, and it's more convenient that way than in the church, since they have heat and towels and everything right there! And you can even have a cup of coffee with them afterward.

Baptism is thus a tremendous object lesson. If we do it at the right time, people understand much better what they are doing. They are escaping from darkness and being born into the Kingdom of God.

4

Living in the Kingdom

"If any one wishes to come after Me, let him deny himself, and take up his cross, and follow Me.

"For whoever wishes to save his life shall lose it; but whoever loses his life for My sake shall find it."
—Matthew 16:24,25

We must flee from darkness and the kingdom of selfishness, where everyone lives for himself and does his own will. We must get into the Kingdom of God, where everyone lives for God and does His will. God's Kingdom must grow and grow and grow, until "the kingdom of this world has become the kingdom of our Lord, and of His Christ" (Revelation 11:15).

To be in the Kingdom, we must die to ourselves. But many people who have been saved don't yet understand that they are slaves. They want to keep on doing their own will. It won't work.

That is why Jesus said you have to lose your life in order to save it. Many people come to the church wanting to save their own lives. But that means ignoring the will of Jesus. And in this Kingdom, He is the Lord.

Jesus said in Matthew 13 that the Kingdom of God was like a merchant looking for fine pearls. And when he found a pearl of great price, he sold everything he had to buy it.

Of course, some Christians think this story means *we* are the pearl of great price and Christ had to give up everything to redeem us. But now we understand that *He* is the pearl of great price. We are the merchants seeking for happiness, for security, for fame, for eternity.

And when we find Jesus, it costs us everything. He has happiness, joy, peace, healing, security, eternity, everything. So we say, "I want this pearl. How much is it?"

"Well," the seller says, "it's very expensive."

"But how much?" we ask.

"Well, a very large amount."

"Do you think I could buy it?"

"Oh, of course. Everyone can buy it."

"But didn't you say it was very expensive?"

"Yes."

"Well, how much is it?"

"Everything you have," says the seller.

We make up our minds. "All right, I'll buy it," we say.

"Well, what do you have?" he wants to know. "Let's write it down."

"Well, I have ten thousand dollars in the bank."

"Good—ten thousand dollars. What else?"

"That's all. That's all I have."

"Nothing more?"

"Well, I have a few dollars here in my pocket."

"How much?"

We start digging. "Well, let's see—thirty, forty, sixty, eighty, a hundred, a hundred twenty dollars."

"That's fine. What else do you have?"

"Well, nothing. That's all."

"Where do you live?" He's still probing.

"In my house. Yes, I have a house."

"The house, too, then." He writes that down.

"You mean I have to live in my camper?"

"You have a camper? That, too. What else?"

"I'll have to sleep in my car!"

"You have a car?"

"Two of them."

"Both become mine, both cars. What else?"

"Well, you already have my money, my house, my camper, my cars. What more do you want?"

"Are you alone in this world?"

"No, I have a wife and two children . . . ."

"Oh, yes, your wife and children, too. What else?"

I have nothing left! I am left alone now."

Suddenly the seller exclaims, "Oh, I almost forgot! *You* yourself, too! Everything becomes mine—wife, children, house, money, cars—and you too."

Then he goes on. "Now listen—I will allow you to use all these things for the time being. But don't forget that they are mine, just as you are. And whenever I need any of them you must give them up, because now I am the owner."

That's how it is when you are under the ownership of Jesus Christ.

When we first began to preach this message of discipleship in Buenos Aires, our congregations were very willing to obey. Many of our members were bringing their homes and apartments to give to the church. (In my country, inflation is so bad that you don't put money in the bank, because you will only fall behind. Instead, you buy something—anything—that has a value that will rise with the inflation. Our apartments are our life savings.)

We didn't know what to do with all these properties. The

pastors met together. One said, "Maybe we should sell all these and use the money to build a big church in the city."

But others said, "No, no, that's not the will of the Lord."

After six months of prayer, the Lord showed us what to do. We called the people together and said, "We are going to return everyone's real estate. The Lord has showed us that He doesn't want your empty houses. He wants a house with you inside taking care of it. He wants the carpets and the heating and the air conditioning and the lights and the food and everything ready—for Him. He also wants your car, with you as the driver.

"Just remember, though, that it all still belongs to Him."

So now all the houses are open. When visitors come to our congregation, we don't say, "Who can take these brothers to your house?"

Instead, we say to someone, "You, brother, you're going to take these people to your house." We don't ask; we command because the house is already given to the Lord. And the people thank the Lord that He lets them live in His house.

It's a completely different approach. But it makes sense once you think of yourself as a slave in the Kingdom of God.

God's Kingdom is also like a marriage. When the woman marries the man, she becomes his. And all his things are hers. If he has a car or two, they are hers.

But in the process, she loses her name.

We have done wrong in the past by not telling people the whole story. We've told them that everything Jesus has becomes theirs, but we forgot to mention that everything we have becomes His. And there's no lordship if we won't do that.

Jesus said, "I would that you were cold or hot. So because you are lukewarm, and neither hot nor cold, I will spit you out of My mouth" (Revelation 3:15-16).

Do you know what that means? Excuse me for this illustration, but it comes from Jesus Himself. What things do we vomit? Things that won't digest. If something is digested, it doesn't come back up.

Vomited people are those people who refuse to be digested by the Lord Jesus Christ.

And digestion means getting lost. You're finished. Your life ends. You are transformed into Jesus. You are unmistakably associated with Him.

In Argentina we have very good steaks. Let's imagine that the steak comes to my stomach, and the gastric juices come along to dissolve it. They say to the steak, "Good evening, how are you?"

The steak replies, "Fine, fine. What do you want?"

"We have come to dissolve you, to transform you in Juan Carlos."

Suppose the steak says, "Oh, no. Wait a minute. It's enough that he ate me. But to disappear completely—no, no, no. I'm in his stomach, but I want to stay steak. I don't want to lose my individuality. I want to maintain my steak citizenship."

"No, sir. You must be dissolved and become Juan Carlos."

"No, I want to stay steak."

So there is a fight. Suppose the steak wins, and the gastric juices let him remain as steak in my stomach.

Very soon that steak will be vomited out.

But if the gastric juices win the fight, the steak loses its personality and becomes Juan Carlos Ortiz. (Before I ate the steak, it was an unknown cow behind the hills. Nobody paid any attention to it. But now, because it is dissolved, it gets to write a book!)

So it is with the Lord. We are "in Christ." It is up to us whether we stay there or not. In order to remain in Jesus, we must lose everything and become Jesus. We lose our life. Like the slave we read about in Luke 17, all our time becomes His—the eight hours we work, the eight hours we sleep, and

37

the other eight hours as well.

Sometimes a Christian says to himself, "Well, now that I'm finished working for the day, I'll go home and take a shower. Then I'll watch television for a while, and then I'll go to bed. Yes, I know there's a meeting tonight, but after all, pastor, I'm entitled to a little rest . . . ."

Entitled to *what,* Mr. Slave? You are entitled to nothing. You are bought by Jesus Christ, and He owns all the hours of your day.

As the slave in Jesus' story finished plowing, he wasn't thinking, *Well, I wonder what snack I can find for myself now.* He was thinking, *What shall I fix for my master? Rice and beans? No, he had that yesterday. A steak with French fries? No, he would like a baked potato better . . . .*

"Well, I think I'll go to church tonight. Who's preaching, darling?"

"Oh, I think So-and-so is going to preach."

"Oh, well, then I think I'll stay home."

We are all upside down. The lords sit in the pews. We treat Jesus as if He were *our* slave. We pray, "Lord" (but our attitude is the opposite), "I'm leaving now. Please watch the house so that no one breaks in while I'm gone. And please keep me from an accident while I drive."

What do we expect Jesus to say?! "Yes, ma'am" or "Yes, sir"?

Servants don't say, "Lord, do this and do that." Servants say, "Lord, what do You want me to do?" The satisfaction of the servant is to see the Lord satisfied. No wonder our churches don't work right. We have not begun to think about how to serve Jesus. Our praises are His dinner. The hymns are the water on His table. The offering is yet another part of His meal.

But we fool ourselves. We say, "Let's raise an offering for the Lord so we can air-condition the church." The Lord doesn't need air conditioning. It's for us. Many of the offerings that we say are for the Lord are really for ourselves.

The only things Jesus talked about as being given to Him were gifts to the poor.

What is Jesus' main dish? Human lives. Paul says in Romans 12:1 that it is a logical service to bring Jesus our bodies. When the Lord sees us bringing another person to Him, He says, "Good. Here comes My servant with My food." Another person becomes dissolved into Jesus.

Jesus concluded His story by saying, "When you do all the things which are commanded you, say, 'We are unworthy slaves; we have done only that which we ought to have done'" (Luke 17:10).

Can you say you have done everything the Lord told you to do? If so, we can have a graduation ceremony for you. We will give you a diploma that reads, "Unworthy Slave."

We are so upside down today that we give unworthy slaves a diploma that reads, "Reverend." Once I was in a meeting where someone was introduced with great fanfare. The organ played and the spotlights came on as someone announced, "And now, the great servant of God,——."

If he was great, he was not a servant. And if he was a servant, he was not great. Servants are people who understand that they are worthy of nothing. They work eight hours and then come in and fix dinner for their Lord—and are refreshed and joyful when they see their Lord enjoying the meal.

May God help us to do with joy what servants in His Kingdom do.

5

The Oxygen of the Kingdom

"A new commandment I give to you, that you love one another, even as I have loved you, that you also love one another.
"By this all men will know that you are My disciples, if you have love for one another."

—John 13:34-35

Before you get too fearful about being a slave, I had better speak about the oxygen of the Kingdom—love.

For many years I thought of love as one of the virtues of the Christian life. In my sermons I told people it was one of the most important things.

Then I began to experience real love. And I found that it is not one of the virtues of the Christian life—love *is* the Christian life. It is not one of the most important things—it is the *one* thing.

When we speak about eternal life, we always seem to think about its length. Years and years and years. We never seem to think about its quality. If eternal life means only never-ending life, then hell is a form of eternal life!

But the quality of eternal life that Jesus gives is love. It is the oxygen; there is no life without it. Love is the only eternal element. The other tremendous elements—gifts, tongues, prophecies, wisdom, knowledge, Bible reading, prayer—will all come to an end. The only thing that will go through death and into the eternal is love.

Love is the light of the new Kingdom. The Bible is so clear when it says that God is light and God is love. John wrote that "if we walk in the light as He Himself is in the light, we have fellowship with one another, and the blood of Jesus His Son cleanses us from all sin" (John 1:7).

I don't know why we have always thought that the light was knowledge. Maybe it's because in English the word *light* sometimes means "a clearer understanding"; you talk about "seeing the light" on something.

But in the Bible, light is love. "The one who loves his brother abides in the light," says 1 John 2:10-11, "... but the one who hates his brother is in the darkness and walks in the darkness, and does not know where he is going because the darkness has blinded his eyes."

What is darkness? Simply the lack of light. We don't have to buy darkness; we don't have to bring in many sacks of darkness to fill a building with it. We simply turn out the light, and it's there.

So it is with the kingdom of darkness. It feels very lonely. In my country we often used to have blackouts in the evening. We would be preaching, and suddenly the lights would go out. What happened? Wives would immediately say to their husbands, "Darling, are you there? Give me your hand."

Things were the same as before, but suddenly people felt alone, even in the company of others.

In the daytime we go everywhere, even to the cemetery with flowers. But we don't go to the cemetery at night. Why? The dead are as dead at night as during the day. But the darkness makes us not want to be there.

Darkness is individualism, selfishness. Light is love, communion, fellowship. If we walk in the light, we have fellowship, because we see each other as brothers.

The verse I quoted above says also that "there is no cause for stumbling" in the one who loves his brother. We Christians stumble over each other all the time. The pastors get tangled up with each other, the congregation does the same, even the denominational leaders—there are always problems and misunderstandings. Sometimes when the Spirit comes to a church in power and conviction we have to confess and confess for weeks and weeks because we have been stumbling so much. We haven't been walking in the light of love.

If one brother is in the light while the other is not, they can still avoid stumbling; one will guide the other. And if both brothers are in the light, how much better! No darkness!

I will go on: Love is the proof of our salvation. Some people think the proof is in how we dress or whether we smoke or whether we do or don't do lots of other things. They may be important, but not as important as love. If we had put the same emphasis on love as we put on tobacco over the years, things would have been different. Love is the proof that we are saved or not.

Listen to what John says: "Beloved, let us love one another, for love is from God; and every one who loves is born of God and knows God. The one who does not love does not know God, for God is love" (1 John 4:7-8).

Do you want to know if you are born of God? Very easy, isn't it?

John also says, "We know that we have passed out of death into life, because we love the brethren. He who does not love abides in death" (1 John 3:14).

Sometimes people come to the pastor and say, "I'm not sure of my salvation. I have doubts about it; how can I be sure?" Here is the test, a very plain one. Do you love the brethren?

If you don't love the brethren you are not saved, according to John's test. You are abiding in death. You can have all the right doctrine on the Tribulation and the Millennium, but the only way to know if you have passed from death to life, from darkness to light, is by your love.

I must go even further (I hope I don't scandalize you): If we loved the way God wanted us to love, we wouldn't have to depend on the commands of the Bible so much. Because "love . . . is the fulfillment of the law" (Romans 13:10). This is what the new covenant is all about: "I will put My law within them, and on their heart I will write it. . . ." (Jeremiah 31:33).

When love is generated from the inside, it solves all kinds of problems. The fruit of the Spirit is love—as well as joy, peace, patience, kindness, goodness, faithfulness, gentleness, and self-control (Galatians 5:22-23). Why do we preach so much? Because we want to build love and these other things in the Christians. But if love were growing as it should, we wouldn't need so many sermons. Love is not one of the elements of the Christian life—it is *the* element. Love is the life itself.

Some people fool themselves by seeking the Spirit's gifts instead of His fruit. Even though we appreciate the gifts, we must be careful where we put the emphasis. Jesus never said, "You will know them by their gifts." He said, "You will know them by their fruits" (Matthew 7:20).

Gifts do not indicate spirituality, because gifts on a person are like gifts on a Christmas tree. In a crowded city like Buenos Aires, we do not have many trees. Most of our Christmas trees are artificial creations of wire and cable and green paper. But we fix them nicely. We buy them for two or three dollars and hang watches and rings and other gifts on them. They look very nice, even though they're not natural trees.

But when you step outside on December 26, all the Christmas trees are in the garbage. They may have carried expensive Omega watches yesterday, but today they are in the garbage. So you can't say much about the tree on the basis of its gifts. The gifts do not indicate what kind of tree it is.

Only by the fruit can you tell something about the tree. If the apples are good, you can say you have a good apple tree, and so forth.

Of course, the best thing would be for a tree to have both good apples and Omega watches, both fruit and gifts. But if that is not possible, at least the fruit should be good. A person may be excused if he doesn't have gifts, but there is no excuse for not having fruit. If we say to the apple tree, "Why don't you have a nice ring on you?" the tree could say, "Excuse me, but no one has put a ring on me." But the apple tree cannot get away without having apples on it, because apples are the result of a normal apple tree.

So we cannot excuse ourselves for not having love. If we are full of the Spirit, the natural thing is for us to be loving.

I am sorry that for so many years we Pentecostals put the emphasis on Acts 2:4 and not on Galatians 5:22. Our statement of faith said, "We believe in the infilling of the Holy Spirit according to Acts 2:4," that is, with speaking in tongues. History would have been different if we had said, "We believe in the infilling of the Holy Spirit according to Galatians 5:22." For one thing, there would not have been so many divisions among Spirit-filled people.

As a Pentecostal minister, it's hard for me to say that. But it's the truth nevertheless, and the Holy Spirit wants us to face it. When you go hunting for deer or some other animal, you aim your rifle at the head, not the tail. Because if you hit him in the head, the whole animal will be yours.

In seeking the infilling of the Holy Spirit, the head is the fruit of the Spirit, and the tail is tongues. Many of us have hit the tail, but the animal kept running. If we had hit the head, we would have had the tail and all.

Jesus did not say, "By this all men will know that you are My disciples, if you speak in tongues." Though I myself speak in tongues, I have to say that the world will know of my discipleship by the sign of love. It is time to place the accent where it belongs, where God has placed it.

Samson had gifts, *charismas*—and he was a carnal man. Saul, the first king of Israel, was a charismatic—he prophesied. But he was a carnal man. Paul said that if he spoke in the tongues of men and of angels, but had no love, it was nothing but noise. Speaking in tongues without love is noise. Prophecy and the ability to understand spiritual mysteries, without love, are nothing. The gift of faith without love is nothing.

So if you see someone manifesting a gift, even raising the dead, don't run after him so quickly. First go nearer to that tree. Don't look at the watches and rings; look under the leaves for the fruit. Especially in these days of confusion, the people of God must be very wise.

Are you really aware of the importance of love? Only if you understand this can you be open to the Spirit. It's like the flour in the cake. You can bake a cake without eggs or salt—but not without flour. Love *is* the Christian life. Many other things such as gifts and worship are nice, but love is the life.

6

Neighbor Love

"You shall love your neighbor as yourself."
—*Leviticus 19:18*

The first degree of love is the minimum, the Old Testament type of love. This is not a commandment only for the church, of course. It is a universal commandment. It is part of God's moral law; if everyone in the world loves someone else, then everyone will be loved and be loving somebody.

What does this command mean? It means that I must wish for my neighbor the same thing I wish for myself. And I must make the same effort to get for my neighbor what I get for myself.

If I have a plate of food and my neighbor doesn't, to love him is to make the same effort to get food for him that I did for myself. If I cannot, then I should give him half of what I

46

have. If I have two suits and he has none, I must make the same effort to get him two suits that I did to get mine. If my children are well-dressed and fed and going to school, and his are not, I must make the same effort for his children that I make for my own.

That is what it means to love your neighbor as yourself. You know something? Most of us believers are not even fulfilling this Old Testament commandment! We are not even loving each other as neighbors.

And of course, Jesus didn't say that we should love each other as neighbors, but as brothers. But if we would at least love each other in the church as neighbors, a revolution would start. In every congregation we have people who have too much and people who have nothing. One believer has a big car and goes home to a big, nice house with turkey and beef waiting. But together they sing about how much they love each other! And when the meeting is over, they say to each other, "God bless you, brother!" and then each goes his way.

When Jesus was asked, "Who is my neighbor?" He answered with the parable of the good Samaritan (Luke 10). So many times I preached about that parable and spiritualized it. Jerusalem was the church. Jericho was the world. The man descending was the believer leaving the church and going to the world. The thieves were Satan and his demons, and the good Samaritan was the brother who brought him back to the church.

Wasn't that a nice way to escape my duty? I was preaching the Fifth Gospel, the Gospel according to the Saint Evangelicals.

Another time I had a different interpretation. Jerusalem was the Garden of Eden, and Jericho was the fall of man, and Jesus was the good Samaritan who came along . . . oh, there are so many ways to preach it.

Jesus finished by telling the lawyer who had asked the question, "Go and do the same" (verse 37). He meant that if we see a person in need, we must meet that need. It's very plain. It doesn't need any spiritualizing.

But we pass by suffering people only to go home and talk about it. "Oh, I saw a terrible sight today—poor fellow, I feel so sorry for him." But we don't do anything.

The Samaritan was nothing special. We have called him the "good Samaritan," but Jesus didn't. He just said, "A certain Samaritan, who was on a journey, came upon him . . ." (verse 33). He was simply obeying the old commandment. He left some money to pay for the man's care, and then went on to do his own business.

But we are so bad that, by comparison, he was a *good* Samaritan. The same thing happens in the churches today. A pastor will say, "Come, Brother Ortiz, I want to introduce you to a very good deacon of mine."

"Oh, I'll be pleased to meet him," I say.

So after we have met, I ask the pastor, "Why did you say he is a good deacon?"

"Well, because he comes to all the meetings. He tithes. He helps me every time I ask him."

That's not a *good* deacon—that's just a deacon! But when a person is close to normal, we say he's "very good."

Wouldn't God be pleased if He could get us all to be normal Samaritans?

Jesus said, "Let your light shine before men in such a way that they may see your good works, and glorify your Father who is in heaven" (Matthew 5:16). What is the light? What is it that produces good works? Love! As I said before, the light of God is love.

Now we must make a concrete application. When we speak about love or anything else in the Bible, we must be specific, or it is like sewing without first making a knot at the end of the thread. You can sew and sew and sew, but things stay the same as they always were. Sometimes we even try to sew without any thread at all—just the needle. All we do is make little holes. But the garment stays torn because we don't take specific steps to conserve our gains.

God does not say, "Love your neighbors." You cannot love the whole world. He says, "Love your neighbor." So take one person, one family. Start to pray for that family. Start to look for their problems, their needs—spiritual, material, psychological, all kinds of needs.

Don't go to them with a tract; you will look like a salesman. Go to sell yourself. Go to give yourself to them. Let them know that you love them, and give your service to them.

We had an older lady in Argentina who, as she put it, "could never win a soul to Jesus." (Actually, we don't believe in winning souls; we believe in winning the soul, body, and spirit—the whole person.) She had been in the church many years. But one day the Lord showed her this type of love. She understood that God didn't send a tract from heaven; He sent His Son, who came and lived with us and healed people. He helped us and shared with us.

The woman decided she could do the same thing.

In front of where she lived was a house for rent. As soon as the new people arrived, she was prepared. She went over with coffee and donuts and said, "I'm bringing you something to eat, because I know you've just moved, and you don't have things ready for cooking yet. I'll come back later to get the dishes—don't bother to wash them, because I know you're busy.

"And by the way, if you want to know about the grocery store, it's at such-and-such a corner . . . ." She didn't put a tract under the donut. She just brought the food and gave them help.

After awhile she came back to get the dishes. She said, "If you need something else, I'm here. If you want anything, I'll be glad to help you."

She never preached about Christ. But a month later the whole family was baptized because of the light she had brought them.

Jesus didn't say, "Let your mouth speak before men in

49

such a way that they may hear your nice words and glorify your Father." He said, "Let your light shine"—your love! Maybe some of us have a problem with this because we were taught such an anti-Catholic gospel. We have removed all importance from good works. We are not saved by works, we say. And that is half the truth. But we *are* "created in Christ Jesus for good works" (Ephesians 2:10).

We read about Cornelius in Acts 10 and all the good things he did—and we like to point out that he still wasn't saved. But notice that God sent him an angel because "your prayers and alms have ascended as a memorial" (verse 4). That's the other half of the truth.

Good works are the evidence of our love. Sometimes we are too mystical—"ohhhhhh, I love you, brother"—but we don't show that we love in any way other than hugging and smiling.

Good works mean good works. Works mean *work*, not just a mystical way of thinking. We must open our wallets and do good works. Of course, there is a difference between good works out of love and good works out of the flesh. Paul says that if I give all my goods to help the poor and have no love, I am nothing. That is why Marxism is not the answer. Marxism has many nice features. Communism says some very good things about social justice and about sharing everything. But it is the opposite of what Jesus taught us. (It's like with spiritism and the gifts of the Spirit—there are similarities, but they come from different sources.)

But listen—in order to be against spiritism, do not deny the gifts. In order to be against communism, do not deny sharing.

Don't forget that we must love our neighbor here and now.

7

Brother Love

"A new commandment I give to you, that you love one another, even as I have loved you, that you also love one another."

—*John 13:34*

The old commandment, the minimum degree of love, was a love with limits. It was based on our love for ourselves. It meant loving my neighbor so long as I am not in danger. But if I am in danger, my love for my neighbor is finished.

That is the minimum. Of course, we think even that is too much—we call it the maximum! Actually, if someone in the church loves me as a neighbor, I should be offended. I'm not his neighbor—I'm his brother! We are not two families living next door to each other—we are part of the same family.

The disciples may have said, "We know about the Ten Commandments, but what is this? This must be the eleventh commandment."

Jesus didn't really care what they called it, just so they obeyed it. "A new commandment I give to you, that you love one another—"

"Yes, we already know that," the disciples said.

"—As I have loved you." Now that was new. What a strange thing.

The old commandment said, "Love your neighbor as you love yourself."

The new commandment said, "Love your brother as I have loved you."

How did Jesus love us? Did He love us as He loved Himself?

No. He loved us *more* than He loved Himself. He gave His life for us.

In this degree of love, self disappears. We must love and love and love until when? Until forever. Even if it costs us our lives. This is much more than giving half the plate of food. It's giving all the plate, and ourselves as well.

This is the degree of love which Jesus meant for the Church, the family of God. It is the love meant to rule our Christian community. I cannot love my brother as I love myself, because self is gone. It is not I who lives, but Jesus.

We have trouble giving ourselves to anyone else, don't we? A great fence keeps us in. That fence is selfishness.

But it must be torn down, or we will never change the Church. Pastors cannot change the structure of the Church from the pulpit. Each of us must change his or her own life structure, which up until now has been based on "I." I am talking about the internal skeletons of our houses, the part you don't see behind the walls and the trim and the face brick.

We sometimes make a lot of changes in our personal houses without changing the structure. We can shut the window that lets in tobacco and open the window to Sunday school. We can shut the window to burlesque theaters and open the window to choir rehearsal. We can shut the window to liquor and open the window to giving money to the church. We can put in new carpeting, new curtains, new wallpaper. But the structure of our houses remains the same; it is still shaped around "I." And problems eventually show up.

Jesus wants more than just new curtains and opened windows; His cross means death to the old structure. He knocks down the whole house and starts over again. There's that gospel song that says, "Leave your heavy burden at the cross/And go free, oh, sinner, go free." That's not enough. Getting rid of the burden of sin is good, but it's not good if the self walks away the same as it was.

We must experience an atomic blast at the cross that not only knocks loose our burden of sin but destroys our "I" structure. It must be replaced with a "C" structure, that is, Christ.

In baptism, it's more than the tobacco, the drinking, and the gambling that stay under the water. It's self. People must understand that. When they come up out of the water, they leave behind themselves. They are completely finished. It is a totally new self which now begins to live a life of obedience, and this must be very plain.

We pastors sometimes say that we should have more fellowship. We should spend time with the Methodist pastor, the Presbyterian pastor, the Catholic priest, and so forth. But then we say, "Oh, but I have no time. I am so occupied with my own ministry."

We are liars. We have time. We have twenty-four hours every day like everyone else does. Why don't we be honest and say, "I have the time, but it's all tied up in myself and my own things"? At least that way we wouldn't be hypocritical about it. We would face our I-centered life for what it is.

Who can obey the new commandment? Who can love his brothers as Jesus loved us?

Well, it must be possible; Jesus must have expected obedience. He gave the commandment for you and me.

We have to make time for loving. A student in our congregation always seemed to be so busy. Every time we approached him about something, he'd say, "Oh, excuse me, pastor, but I have no time. I'm studying and I'm also working eight hours a day. So you can imagine how I can't do anything more than that. I can make the meetings once a week, but the rest of the time I'm occupied."

Then one day he fell in love. Suddenly he had time to visit his girlfriend three or four times a week.

How did he do it? I don't know. Love did it.

When we say we have no time, we are showing our own selfishness. We mean that all our time is involved in building our own little kingdom. But if we were to die, we'd have all the time we needed for others. Jesus had twenty-four hours each day for other people. He had no personal things to do. Why? Because He was bearing a cross on His shoulders, and He said that His followers had to do the same.

Do you know what it means to take the cross? Some people think the cross is to have their mother-in-law come for a visit. That's not the cross. When a Jew saw somebody in the street with a cross on his shoulder, he knew what was going to happen. The person was going to die.

Jesus said to take up your cross and live like a dead person. Are you ready? Are you prepared at any time for the cross to be put on the floor and you be nailed to it? If you are, you won't have any trouble with the new commandment.

Everyone knows John 3:16. But did you ever notice 1 John 3:16? Probably not—this verse is not in the Gospel according to the Saint Evangelicals. It reads, "We know love by this, that He laid down His life for us; and we ought to lay down our lives for the brethren."

This verse is not in the little promise boxes. If it were, no one would buy them! The people who make up promise boxes always include the nicest verses, so Christians can pull out a card and say, "Oh, look what the Lord is going to do for me!"

I would have great fun making one of those boxes using all the verses not underlined in our Bibles. Verses like 1 John 3:16—wouldn't that be a surprise!

The apostle John has once again come up with a very simple test for us. Do we know love? It's very easy to tell; you don't need the gift of discerning spirits or anything. Just ask yourself whether you're willing to lay down your life for your brother. Think of a specific brother in your congregation. Would you die for him?

I have friends who have told me, "Juan, I have given my life to God for your sake. If something happens to you, it happens to me. So my life is in your hands. If you need my blood, it's yours. So is my car, my home, everything." This is the new commandment kind of love.

God is going to have a new community. Things are starting to happen in the church. The world generally doesn't know it yet, but it's coming. We are going to be like a city on a mountain, an example of a community that loves one another.

Where does it start? This love must begin among the preachers of love. The pastors have always been more divided, more concerned about their differences, than the people. So we must set the example in every city by creating a fellowship among the pastors of the city. We cannot get our congregations to love if we do not. After all, we are the shepherds.

Every pastor has many sermons on love. Now we must practice what we have been preaching.

The sheep want to be together. They are tired of division. We, the leaders, are the problem. We must be baptized in love before Jesus comes again. We must be the examples of love for the flock.

Pastors sometimes tell me, "Yes, I know. I know the doctrine of the unity of the church. And I've invited the other pastors to meetings. I've sent each one of them a letter, but they haven't come."

That's the wrong way to start. Pastors are tired of meetings. They are also threatened by them. If someone introduces you to a young girl, you cannot say, "Hello, nice to meet you—come on, let's get married." You must first fall in love. So you must first fall in love with the other pastors before you invite them to the courthouse to get married to you.

Actually, a meeting is not usually held for fellowship anyway. If a meeting is scheduled for 8:00, the pastors will arrive at 7:59. They will all say hello to each other and then sit and look at the back of one another's heads. When the meeting is over, they will say good-by and be out the door.

Where is the fellowship?

We have the same problem, by the way, among the sheep. Christians can come together and say, "Hello, how are you? Give my regards to your family" every Sunday for twenty years and never go any deeper. The structure of our meetings doesn't allow for fellowship or showing love.

Have you ever seen a boyfriend who said to his girl, "Hello, how are you? How is your family? Well, it's time to say good-by." No—they grow and grow in fellowship until they cannot do anything but get married.

This is what must happen among the pastors of each city. Their whole spirits and souls must be awakened to love one another as Jesus loved us.

So we don't start with meetings. We start by saying, "Lord, I will make time to love two or three pastors in my city. I will write down their names here. I don't even know them now; I have opposed their theology. But now I will love them, because love is a commandment."

(Someone will say, "Brother, you are right—love is a commandment, but if God doesn't give us this love, then we can't do it."

(Aren't we smart? God tells us to do something, and we work things around so we hand it right back to Him. We pray, "God, give me love for my brother." And then we think that if we don't love, it's not our fault—God didn't answer our prayer!

56

(Listen—love is a commandment. We don't need to ask where the love will come from. We just need to start obeying our Lord. When we obey, things will happen.)

How do I fall in love with the two or three pastors on my list?

First, I start to pray for them every day for a week or two. I find out if they have families and relatives; I learn their names and pray for them. I pray for the wife and for the children in school. I drive past the house and say, "Lord Jesus, bless that home."

And when I finally fall in love with them—I go to see them. With my heart full of love, I knock on the door.

"Hello, is this the home of Pastor Smith?"

"Yes, I'm Pastor Smith."

"Well, I'm Pastor Ortiz, and I came to visit you."

He looks surprised, but that's all right. "Well, come on inside," he says. "Why did you come to visit?"

"Well, I just came to visit you, brother," I say.

"Well, I am sort of busy today, so tell me what's on your mind—the main reason why you stopped by."

"The main reason I came was just that I wanted to see you. I know you're busy, so I'll just spend five minutes with you. How were your meetings last Sunday?"

How can he refuse to answer that? He says, "We had a pretty good day. I felt pleased with my sermon, people responded to the message, and the offering was good—almost two thousand dollars last Sunday. So we're doing very well."

"Oh, that's great," I say. "Do you have a family?"

"Yes, a wife and three children. My wife is sick at the moment."

I stand up. "Oh, I'm sorry to hear that. I'll be on my way now, but let's pray before I leave. 'Thank you, Jesus, for this house, for this brother, for the meeting they had, for his wife. Heal her and help her. Amen.' Thank you so much, Pastor Smith. Good-by."

As he closes the door of his house, he says to himself,

Poor man. I'd better call his bishop. Perhaps he's over-worked.

"Hello, is this the bishop? Pastor Ortiz belongs to your denomination, I believe . . . yes, he came to my house today. Have you noticed anything strange about him the past few days? I don't think he's well. You know, pastors work so hard that sometimes their minds sort of crack. . . . Yes, please keep your eye on him. He came here for nothing—imagine that! . . . Uh huh, well, I'm sure you'll take care of him. Good-by."

The next week, Pastor Ortiz is back knocking on the door. Pastor Smith looks out the window and says, "Oh—the crazy one! But at least he doesn't stay long." So he opens the door.

Good morning. Pastor Ortiz. How are you?"

"Very well, Pastor Smith."

"What do you want?"

"Well, I just came to visit you." He already knows he must invite me in. Then I say:

"How is your wife? You know, my wife and I were praying all last week for her, and my wife wanted to come visit her, but she wasn't sure if she was well enough to receive visitors or not. But she sent this little gift anyway."

"Well, thank you so much. Tell your wife she may certainly come if she wants to."

"How was your meeting last Sunday?"

"Fine—we had a nice meeting."

"Well, brother, let's pray, and I'll be on my way. 'Thank you, Jesus, that this brother's wife is better. Amen.' Good-by!"

The next week, again I knock at the door. By the fifth week . . . he's waiting for me!

But the next step is still not to invite him to a meeting. I invite him to play golf or to come to my home for ice cream. He may be against my denomination, but he cannot be against ice cream. I *love* him. After we play golf together, after he comes to my house, after he invites me and my wife to his house, we are friends. I have gained his confidence.

Then I share with him my burden for the pastors of the city to truly be brothers and love each other. Love is the horse that pulls the cart of brotherhood. Don't put the horse behind the cart. First love, *then* share your feelings.

Is this too hard? Jesus said we ought to lay down our lives for the brethren. To go and visit a brother pastor is much less than giving my life. This is just the beginning.

Once it starts with us pastors, it will spread quickly to the other parts of the Body of Christ in our cities. But it must begin with us. We must have the eyes of Jesus. When Jesus looks at your city, He sees His shepherds and His sheep as all one unit. If we are in Jesus, we will see the same thing. Not all of us have the "right" doctrine. But that doesn't seem to stop Jesus from loving us anyway. Neither should it stop Jesus' servants.

There was a man in my former denomination who became my enemy some time ago. He said I was not being faithful to the church. Eventually he started to hate me.

During one of the conventions I went to him and said, "Hello, how are you?" and gave him a hug.

"Don't hug me— I don't love you," he growled.

"Well, I love you," I replied.

"You cannot love me, because I'm your enemy!" He was almost shouting.

"Praise the Lord!" I said. "I didn't know that you were my enemy, but here's an opportunity for me to love my enemies. 'Thank You, Jesus, for my precious enemy!' "

You know something? One year later I was preaching in his church.

Love is the most powerful weapon in the world. Jesus conquers the world by love, and so do we.

8

Mashed Potato Love

"... I have made Thy name known to them, and will make it known; that the love wherewith Thou didst love Me may be in them, and I in them."

—*John 17:26*

The third degree of love goes beyond both the old and new commandments. It is the Trinity type of love.

Can you imagine the love among the Trinity? Can you imagine how the Father loves the Son? How the Son loves the Father? How the Spirit loves the Son? How the Spirit loves the Father? How the Father loves the Spirit? How the Son loves the Spirit? Tremendous!

This is eternal love. It is the love for mature people. This degree of love assures that there will never be a disagreement. In the Old Testament we read how the Father did miracles and wonders, raised the dead, and healed the sick. Then the Son came to earth and did the same things. The Father was not envious of that; He said He was "well pleased" (Matthew 17:5).

Then the Holy Spirit came and began doing the same things. Still there was complete unity. Their love is so mature that nothing offends them.

The Trinity type of love makes three to be one. Two plus eternal love equals one! Three plus eternal love equals one. Four plus eternal love equals one.

And a hundred Christians plus eternal love equals one. It works with any number.

Jesus prayed that this degree of love "may be in them," meaning us.

When I was a boy in Sunday School, the teacher spoke one week about how we are in Christ. I understood that.

But then another week he said Christ is in us. I said, "You must be wrong. If we are in Christ, how can Christ be in us at the same time? If one thing is inside another, the bigger thing cannot be inside the smaller at the same time."

But now it is very easy to understand. If I am in my brother's heart and he is in my heart, we are both in the other. We are one because of love.

Obviously today we are not one. We are in many groups. We are Methodists, Presbyterians, Pentecostals of many kinds, Nazarenes, Salvation Army, Episcopalians, Plymouth Brethren, Baptists of many kinds, and others as well.

God is regrouping us. He has already begun. He is not using our categories, however, God has only two groups—those who love one another and those who don't.

So if you ask me, "Brother Ortiz, what group are you from?" I will say, "I'm from the group that loves one another." That's the difference between the sheep and the goats that Jesus told about in Matthew 25. We have many sheep in Argentina, and it's interesting to see what happens when you try to move a flock of sheep. They all head in the same direction; they become one body.

But if you try the same thing with goats, they all begin to butt each other and fight.

So it's very easy to tell a sheep from a goat. You don't need the gift of interpretation or discernment or anything. You just talk to the person one or two minutes. If he fights, he's a goat. If he loves, he's a sheep.

How did Jesus separate the sheep from the goats? On the basis of whether they had given water to the thirsty, food to the hungry, companionship to the sick and the prisoners, and so forth. He called the people who had shown love to their brothers "blessed of My Father" (verse 34). The others were called the opposite, the "accursed ones" (verse 41).

But listen—God is doing even more than regrouping His people. He is uniting them. I can illustrate this with potatoes. Each potato plant in the garden has three, four, or five potatoes under it. Each individual potato belongs to one plant or another.

When the harvest comes, all the potatoes are dug up and put into one sack. So they are regrouped. But they are not yet united. They may say, "Oh, praise the Lord! Now we are all in the same sack." But they are not yet one.

They must be washed and peeled. They think they are closer yet. "How nice is this love among us!" they say.

But that's not all. They must be cut in pieces and mixed. They have now lost a lot of their individuality. They really think they are ready for the Master now.

But what God wants is mashed potatoes. Not many potatoes—one mashed potato. No potato can stand up and say, "Here I am! I'm a potato." The word must be *we*. That's why the Lord's Prayer begins, "*Our* Father which art in heaven . . . ," not "*My* Father which art in heaven . . . ."

With all the reverence possible, I say to you that the

Father, Son, and Holy Spirit are three potatoes made into mashed potatoes. And Jesus is hungry for mashed potatoes. He is going to have them. He is already doing something very profound in His church.

You know something? Very shortly, if we start to love one another in this mature way, the word *brother* can drop out of our vocabulary. As it is now, we have to call each other brother because we don't live as brothers. In my home I was called Skinny. No one had to prove anything by calling me Brother Juan Carlos; everyone knew I was their brother.

In the church we say Pastor Smith or Brother Ortiz because we have no relationship. But we want to appear that we do.

I went to a formal church one time and heard the pastor say, "Mr. Brown, would you lead us in prayer?"

I thought, *How worldly these people are! He doesn't even say Brother Brown.*

Then I found that the relationship between the misters in that church was the same as the relationship between the brothers in mine. We were fooling ourselves with words.

In all our talking about love, let us remember its two dimensions: the mystical and the pragmatic. Mysticism says, "Ohhh, brother, I can just *feeeeel* the love for you." Pragmatism says, "Brother, how much do you need?"

Not long ago I was in a convention in Cordoba, Argentina, where the Lord's Supper was held. The leaders said, "We will not have any preaching today. Instead we have reserved several hours just for the Lord's Supper. We bought twenty pounds of bread—after all, the Bible doesn't say how small or large the portions should be. So we will give each group of four people a whole loaf to break and share as they wish."

We were eating bread for more than an hour in that auditorium. We were hugging and crying, and after awhile the dollar bills were flying all over the place as pragmatic needs were met through love during the Lord's Supper.

Love is a commandment. Love is the oxygen of the Kingdom. Love is the life.

9

The Language of the Kingdom

Praise Him for His mighty deeds.
—*Psalm 150:2*

Of all the Bible people, David is the one who can teach us about praise and worship. More than anyone else, he speaks with authority on how to express the Kingdom love we have inside.

Not long ago, I decided to read his Psalms all at one sitting. I was not looking for special quotations or lines of comfort or encouragement; I wanted to learn something about the man himself, because I wanted to be like him.

I found that his book is arranged like a symphony. It begins very softly. You feel like you felt the first time you heard a philharmonic orchestra. You saw all the instruments there and thought you would be overwhelmed by the sound.

Then just two or three violins began to play. What a disappointment! Then came the piano. Then the mezzo piano. Then the mezzo forte. Then the forte. And by the time all the instruments were playing, you were almost frightened.

The 150th Psalm is David's fortissimo, his grand finale.

> Praise Him with trumpet sound.
> Praise Him with harp and lyre.
> Praise Him with timbrel and dancing.
> Praise Him with stringed instruments and pipe.
> Praise Him with loud cymbals.
> Praise Him with resounding cymbals.
> Let everything that has breath praise the Lord.
> Praise the Lord! (verses 3-6).

Why all this noise? Because of "His mighty deeds."

I was born and raised in a church that emphasized praising the Lord. I learned the words very early. But I didn't learn the *concept* of praise very well, even though a lot of time in our services was given to "praising the Lord."

What is praise? Any dictionary will tell you that it is the recognition of virtues.

It is more than just using the word *praise*. If I am in a meeting where someone sings well, and I go to him afterward and say, "Oh, I praise you, I praise you, I praise you—" that's not praise. I have to praise him *for something*. I should say, "Listen, as you began to sing, my heart really responded to your message. I looked at the faces of the other people, and we were all caught up with your song."

If I see a lady walking down the street with her child, and I run up and grab her hand and say, "Oh, lady, I praise you, I praise you, I praise you!" she will say, "You're crazy!"

But if I say, "Excuse me—are you the mother of this child?" She will say, "Yes."

And I will say, "What a lovely child! Your boy has very nice manners, and you can be proud of him." I have praised her, even though I haven't used the word at all."

If I approach an artist and say, "Oh, I praise you, hallelujah, hallelujah!" he will run the other way.

I should say, "I've been noticing your painting here, and the way you've portrayed the hand with the cup—it's wonderful. It looks almost as if the hand is reaching out of the frame and inviting me to sit down and eat."

How much of our praise to God uses the word *praise*—but doesn't say anything?

Our words have become like empty boxes. In order to teach my congregation about this, I began to question them. When someone said, "Praise the Lord!" I said, "Wait a minute—why do you praise the Lord?"

"Well, I praise the Lord because ahhh, because, well, ahhh . . . ." He didn't know!

Someone else said, "Alleluia!"

And I asked, "Why did you say 'Alleluia'?"

"Well, I said 'Alleluia' because ahhh, um, ahhh . . . ."

"You said 'Alleluia' because you're a Pentecostal and it's part of our liturgy, that's why!"

David said, "Praise Him for His mighty deeds." We haven't done that.

We have come to church with wheelbarrows full of beautifully wrapped boxes tied with nice ribbons and big cards reading, "Praise the Lord!" "Alleluia!" "Glory to God!" and "Amen!"

And the pastors have said, "What wonderful people! They come to church with so much praise."

And all the boxes have been brought to the altar.

But when God has opened His presents, He's found nothing inside.

I once said to myself, *I've been in the church more than thirty years now since I was born. What have I learned in all this time about praise?*

Well, I had learned how to say four things: "Alleluia," "Praise the Lord," "Glory to God," and "Amen." In thirty years!

I had also learned how to shout those four things.

And then recently I had advanced beyond the oldtimers—I had learned how to *sing* those four things. The words were still the same, but now I was singing them, and I thought I was really something.

I said, "Lord, is that all the praise I can give You?"

Then I read what David had written: "Praise Him for His mighty deeds." And I understood that each praise should be because of something. We must know *why* we praise the Lord. Otherwise we deceive ourselves, thinking we are praising the Lord when really we are only mouthing some words.

Suppose I go out shopping. When I come home, my wife says, "Where were you?"

"Shopping."

"What did you buy?"

"Oh, nothing. I was shopping, but I didn't buy anything."

I may use the word *shopping,* but I didn't shop. I just walked around.

Many of us use the word *praise;* we use it a lot. But we aren't praising. God doesn't want words; He wants praise. He doesn't care about the box; He wants what's inside.

My congregation had gone along with my first questions, so I went on to something more. "In order to grow in praising," I announced, "we are going to forbid the four praise phrases for one month in our meetings. We will keep on giving God our praise, but we will find other words to use."

Nobody knew how to praise! My wife said, "Juan, if I can't say, 'Alleluia,' what am I supposed to say? After all, the angels say, 'Alleluia.' "

"Yes," I told her, "they say, 'Hallelujah! For the Lord our God, the Almighty, reigns' " (Revelation 19:6). They praise Him for His mighty deeds. You must have a mighty deed in mind when you praise—otherwise, it is empty."

We had become like the trucks in my country that get

68

stuck on the mud roads. They bog down in one place. They grind away and make lots of noise and use up lots of gasoline—but they don't go anywhere.

I had the same problem—I was making lots of noise, but I was stuck. I had no words. I recognized my poverty in praise, and I said, "Lord, I guess You don't mean very much in my heart. If I don't sing the Psalms of David or else the hymns from the book, I don't have much to tell You."

We learned a lot from that experiment. We found that we had been judging our meetings by the amount of praising that we heard, which often didn't mean a thing. I started trying to find things in my life and experience for which I could praise the Lord. And I found God in many places where I never thought He would be.

I started to see Christ in my brother. At first, all I could think of was "Praise the Lord because he has a pleasant face"! But then I began to think how Jesus lives inside him.

And eventually I realized that praise is more than just an outburst of words on Sunday morning. Praise is an entire language. Praise is the language of the Kingdom of God. As Spanish is the language of Argentina, and English is the language of the United States and Britain, and Portuguese is the language of Brazil, so praise is the language of the Kingdom of God. Citizens of that Kingdom speak its language, and we recognize each other by our accent.

As David put it, "His praise shall continually be in my mouth" (Psalm 34:1). He praised the Lord from his bed as well as during the day.

As far as God is concerned, there are only two languages in this world: the language of His Kingdom and the language of the kingdom of darkness. The first is the language of praise. The second is the language of complaint. Praise recognizes virtue. Complaint criticizes virtue. And every human being speaks one language or the other.

Listen to the citizens of the kingdom of darkness:

The alarm goes off in the morning. "Ohhhh! Who invented work?"

They get to the breakfast table. "The coffee is too hot."

They complain about the weather, the President, the traffic—everything. It's a whole language.

It was quite a shock for me to realize that citizens of the Kingdom of God speak the wrong language most of the time. They go to church and sing, "Alleluia, alleluia"—and then step outside after the meeting and say, "Ugh—it's raining. What an ugly day."

Who made that day? The Lord.

Maybe they should revise their chorus so they could sing, "This is the day that the Lord hath made/We will criticize and complain in it."

How can we sing, "Praise the Lord!" and then criticize the same Person a few minutes later? Our praise is not intelligent. We don't know what we're doing.

Americans sometimes come up to me and say, "Como esta usted?"

And I say, "Muchas gracias, muy bien y usted?"

Then they laugh and say, "Ah, well, I don't know that much Spanish."

Spanish is not really their language; they just learned a few words at school. They quickly run out of things to say.

So it is with some Christians. Their language is not really the language of praise; they can only repeat a few words they learned at the Pentecostal school: "Alleluia!" "Praise the Lord!" But the rest of the day they speak the language of complaining.

If the day is cold or hot instead of raining, we still criticize. "What a horrible day!"

Nothing God made is horrible. The rain is a manifestation of His mighty power. So is the snow and the heat and the ice. I've learned to say, "What a nice sunny day," "What a nice rainy day," "What a nice snowy day," "What a nice hot day"—why not?! All of them are nice, because God made them, and He deserves to be praised for them.

Paul told Timothy, "Everything created by God is good, and nothing is to be rejected, if it is received with gratitude" (1 Timothy 4:4). If we have a thankful heart, everything is good. If not, everything is always wrong.

In Buenos Aires it sometimes gets to be 110 degrees in the summertime. So when it is only 90 or 95, someone will meet me and say, "Hello, Pastor Ortiz. How are you standing the heat?"

"Very well, thank you," I say. "And you?"

"Oh, it's terrible."

"Oh, no, brother—our Father has just turned up the thermostat!"

When it gets up to 100, people complain even more. But the Christian can be proud of his Father. What power He has! It takes huge furnaces to heat a shopping center; our Father can heat the whole country to 110 degrees, and He doesn't even have an office!

Or He can turn things very cold and kill all the germs without using DDT. Fantastic!

A team of Russian skaters comes to my city once each year, and I've seen the huge machines they must bring in to create the smooth ice in the stadium.

But I have also seen God freeze all of Canada! Without any machines! That's the power of God. Praise the Lord for the ice and snow!

Paul also said, "I urge that entreaties and prayers, petitions and thanksgivings, be made on behalf of all men" (1 Timothy 2:1). In one of our meetings when we were trying to praise the Lord without using the four phrases, the Spirit seemed to take control of me, and I said, "Lord, we are going to thank You for some individual people. We will start with the telephone—we take it for granted, but how many technicians are behind it all? Thank You, Lord, for the telephone company."

And all the people said, "Thank You, Lord, for the telephone company."

"Lord, we open the water faucet," I went on, "and out comes water, both cold and hot. We take it for granted. But how many thousands of people work to provide us with that water? Thank You, Lord, for the water company."

Again the people answered, "Yes, Lord, we thank You."

We went on to thank the Lord for the schoolteachers, the bus drivers, the doctors, the nurses, the police, even the mayor of the city. We never did that before! We were too busy saying, "Alleluia!" "Glory to God!" But not having those words, we had to find others. And we entered a new dimension of praise.

I believe God is tired of listening to complaints. When we said, "God, we thank You for the good things the mayor has done," I think God said, "At last! Somebody finally recognized that I caused something good for once."

The one day the telephone doesn't work, we complain, but we forget all the days it works fine. We criticize the pastor the day he doesn't preach too well, but we forget all the good times.

Even when someone dies—why should we be sad and forget all the years he lived?

I had to minister at the funeral of a seventy-year-old woman. I didn't want to use the language of darkness, so I went in and said, "Praise the Lord for the seventy years that this woman was with us! Isn't God good? He gave her to us for such a long time. Let's thank Him for that."

The whole atmosphere changed. Even the husband said, "Thank You, Lord for giving my wife to me for so long." He eventually asked us all to sing a chorus—it would be translated something like this:

> I come to tell You,
> I come to tell You, my Savior and Lord,
> That I love You,
> That I love You with all my heart!

Oh, I'm so glad,
I am so glad and full of joy!

That's hardly a funeral song, but that was what he wanted us to sing. Soon we took hands and began to dance— even the husband. He was so glad for the revelation that the Lord had given his wife seventy years that he wanted to make a feast, a celebration.

Why not?

We must check ourselves to see if we are speaking the wrong language. If we speak the language of the Kingdom of God, we will be praising the Lord every day all through the year, and fully understanding what we're saying.

10

Open Eyes

When I consider Thy heavens,
*   the work of Thy fingers,*
The moon and the stars,
*   which Thou hast ordained;*
What is man, that thou dost
*   take thought of him?*
And the son of man,
*   that Thou dost care for him?*

—Psalm 8:3,4

Let the sea roar and all it contains,
The world and those who dwell in it.
Let the rivers clap their hands;
Let the mountains sing together for joy
Before the Lord . . . .

—Psalm 98:7-9a

The mighty deeds of God are everywhere. Our trouble is that we don't see them. Here is a very childish "revelation" which came to me one day: Maybe the reason we don't have praises to give God is that we try to praise Him with our eyes closed. What can we think of when everything is dark? (Usually, only the four phrases.)

But when we open our eyes and look around, we find all kinds of things to thank the Lord for.

Once my group of disciples and I went on a retreat to a place two hours out of Buenos Aires, a very nice house in a park with pine trees, flowers, and birds. We began praying under an apple tree. It was September, which in my country is springtime.

The first person prayed, "Lord, we come to You today..." and he sounded just like he always did in the basement of our downtown church. The second one did the same.

When it came my turn to pray, I said, "Lord, we drove a long time to be here. If we wanted the same kind of prayer meeting like we always have in the church basement, we could have stayed in Buenos Aires."

I opened my eyes. The apple tree was full of flowers, and a little bird was sitting right there in the middle of it. I went on. "Lord, what fools we are to come so far to this park and then sit with our eyes shut. Lord, how beautiful this apple tree is. The flowers are just fantastic. Look at the bird You have made, Lord. Isn't it beautiful?"

The other men began to open their eyes to see what was happening to their pastor! I kept going.

"Lord, look at those roses. Look at the pine trees.... Now I understand why we haven't had new words for praising. Now I understand why David praised so much—Lord, where in the Bible does it say we must close our eyes to pray?"

I did a quick dash in my mind from Genesis to Revelation—I didn't find any such rule. It's not there. In fact, the Bible shows the opposite; Psalm 121 says, "I will lift up my eyes to the mountains." Jesus began His last prayer by "lifting up His eyes to heaven" (John 17:1). Our tradition has again put us upside down to the Bible.

Well, the other men opened their eyes, and soon they began to pray a second time. One said, "Look, the sun! Isn't it wonderful? Isn't that a miracle of God? Father, You're tremendous! You make things so perfect."

We started to walk around the park. We smelled the roses and talked about the wonderful power of God. One boy climbed a tree and began exclaiming, "All the wonderful things I see from this tree!" He began naming them off.

Soon we all were in the trees (it was a very unusual prayer meeting), shouting like a bunch of monkeys. "Look at that cow! Look at the corn growing by the power of God! Look at that man over there! Look at that couple in love! Praise the Lord for love!"

Then we came down, and soon someone said, "Look at this grass."

"What about the grass?" I said. "Haven't you seen grass before?"

"Yes," he answered, "but now I understand that this is the carpet God has made for all the world. Praise the Lord for His carpet!"

We ran around like this for four hours. It was the most useful prayer meeting we ever had.

Since that day we have prayed with our eyes open, and we've entered a whole new world of praise.

It has changed our entire Pentecostal form of worship. We used to have all kinds of shaking and shouting and carrying on in our meetings. Our eyes were closed, and so we forgot that other people were present. Now all those things are finished. We don't have faces of agony like we used to when we prayed. We realize that other people are watching, and so we put on a nice face!

We even stopped changing our voice and vocabulary for prayer. So many Christians have a whole different way of speaking when they pray; it's very dramatic and flowery. Why? Because they close their eyes and think they've entered another world.

But with our eyes open, we realize that we must live only one kind of life twenty-four hours a day. Everything must be done in God's presence; His is always here. We don't need to put on any special speech for Him.

We even had to rearrange the benches in our church. When they were in rows, we were always looking at the back of other people's heads. But now we wanted to see faces. So we put the benches in circles. And we seem to have more communion. We watch the person praising the Lord and we say, "God, thank You for that man . . . ."

It is true that sometimes we need to close our eyes and look deep inside ourselves. But when we praise God, we are reaching outside, and we find many more things with which to fill our praise boxes as we look around.

Isn't that what David did? He saw a shepherd coming along the road, and he probably said, "Hello. Where are you taking this flock?"

The shepherd may have answered, "To the green pasture and quiet water on the other side of the hill."

And David, being a spiritual man who spoke the language of the Kingdom, saw the beauty of God in that. As he walked on alone, he said to himself:

> The Lord is my shepherd,
> I shall not want.
> He makes me lie down in green pastures;
> He leads me beside quiet waters . . .(Psalm 23:1-2).

If we carnal Christians had been there instead of David, we would have missed the whole point. We would have said, "Hello, shepherd. Tell me, how much wool does each sheep give in a season?"

"Thirty pounds."

"Ah. And how much do you get for each pound?"

"Ten dollars."

"I see—so you can figure on $300 per sheep, right? Good business!"

Nothing but materialism. Yet we go to church and keep singing. "Alleluia! Praise the Lord!"

And the Lord says to Himself, *Hmmm. Same old record again.*

David said, "O sing to the Lord a new song" (Psalm 98:1). If he had been like modern songwriters, he would have been interested in selling his book of songs. "Sing my nice music always!"

But David wanted each person to make up his own psalms. Psalms are not limited to the book between Job and Proverbs. Psalms are the spontaneous reaction of the spiritual man to any given circumstance. If something very bad happens (as often happened to David), our reaction should be a psalm unto the Lord. If we receive good news, the same thing.

Paul told the Ephesians that Spirit-filled people will speak "to one another in psalms" (5:19). Not necessarily the Psalms of David. We don't need to know how to read! But the Spirit inside us can give rise to new psalms of our own making.

How often we sing "borrowed" praises. We use the Psalms of David, but without his attitude. If he were here, he would probably come up, jerk the book out of our hands, and say, "Don't sing like that! I didn't write that Psalm to be sung while you are daydreaming. My heart was full of the things I was telling; it was an outburst of my soul. But you sing so calmly—you're bored!"

Borrowing is all right, but new songs to the Lord are better. Remember what happened when Mary went to visit Elizabeth? What would be the conversation between two expecting ladies in our church? "How many months are you?" "How are you feeling?" "Do you want a boy or a girl?" "Do you have enough clothing?"

But when Mary met Elizabeth, the salutation was a psalm: "Blessed among women are you, and blessed is the fruit of your womb!" (Luke 1:42).

How did Mary respond? With a psalm. "My soul exalts the Lord, and my spirit has rejoiced in God my Savior . . ." (verse 46 and following).

Simeon was another Spirit-filled person. When he saw the Baby, he didn't say, "How nice—how old is your child?" He said: "In peace, according to Thy word; For mine eyes have seen Thy salvation . . ." (Luke 2:29 and following).

Anna the prophetess did the same thing.

Why shouldn't people who are filled with the Spirit have a natural outflowing of psalms?

One day I shut myself in my office and said, "Lord, today I'll sing You a new song." I took my guitar and began strumming. "Alleluia . . . alleluia . . . praise the Lord . . . ." It was pretty weak. I discovered my poverty. I had nothing beyond the borrowed praises I knew from David and Mary and Charles Wesley.

But I kept at it, and since then I have learned to tell God in psalms how much He means to me. Many times my disciples and I have sung new songs to the Lord, speaking and answering each other in turn.

A few years ago my wife and I were traveling alone in Europe for a whole month. When we finally got to Rome, we had lots of letters waiting from my secretary, my mother and the children.

Naturally, we opened the children's mail first. The six-year-old had written all the words he knew how to spell: momma, papa, uncle, cow, horse. It wasn't a real letter, but it was the best he could do, and we were ecstatic. "Look at this!" we said to each other. "How nice!"

The five-year-old did not know how to write, so he had drawn a picture of a wedding, the bride, the bridegroom— and I was the pastor. "Look what he has done!" we exclaimed. We were laughing and exulting and feeling so homesick to see them.

Then we got to the little wrinkled paper from the three-year-old. It was a scribble! "Look at this!" I shouted. My wife started to cry, and soon I was crying.

The Italian pastor who had brought the mail just stared at us. I shoved the pieces of paper in front of his face. "Aren't they wonderful?!"

Why didn't he respond? Because these were not his children. As far as my wife and I were concerned, they were the most precious pieces of paper in the world. We still have them at home.

Listen to me: Go ahead and sing a new song to the Lord—*even if it is a scribble.* He will love it more than Handel's "Hallelujah Chorus" sung by the Mormon Tabernacle Choir. Start to sing. Put the attitude of your heart into new words and a new song. Tell the Lord a story about what has happened to you today, about something you see around you, about anything that shows His power and glory.

God will create such a scene in heaven that the angels will stare at Him just like the Italian pastor. "Listen to this!" God will shout. "Listen to Juan Carlos with his guitar. Yesterday all he sang was 'Alleluia, praise the Lord,' but today he's adding new words. Listen!"

The angel philharmonic orchestra and chorus can do much better, but God says, "I'm tired of all that. Let me hear Johnny scribble a little while."

Fill your empty boxes with new words and new songs. Praise Him for His mighty deeds.

PART TWO

THE NEW WINESKINS

I have the strong feeling that everything I have written up to this point is only talk unless a root problem is faced. I call it the "permanent childhood" of the believer.

What good is it to speak of recognizing Christ as Lord, or of serving Him as a slave, or of putting love and praise into mature action in His new Kingdom—unless we are able to *change,* to *grow* and *move on* from the baby days which we have so prolonged?

That is what the second part of this book is about.

11

A Child Forever?

*... We have much to say, and it is hard to explain, since
you have become dull of hearing.*

*For though by this time you ought to be teachers, you have
need again for some one to teach you the elementary principles of the oracles of God, and you have come to need milk
and not solid food.*

*For every one who partakes only of milk is not ac-
customed to the word of righteousness, for he is a babe.*

*But solid food is for the mature, who because of practice
have their senses trained to discern good and evil.*

*Therefore leaving the elementary teaching about the
Christ, let us press on to maturity, not laying again a foun-
dation of repentance from dead works and of faith toward
God,*

*of instruction about washings, and laying on of hands,
and the resurrection of the dead, and eternal judgments.*

And this we shall do, if God permits.

—Hebrews 5:11-6:3

The Lord really shocked me when He first showed me
how childish my congregation and I were.

When I came to the church in Buenos Aires, it had 184 members. We got to work right away, and after two years of vigorous organizing and outreach, we were up to around 600. We had tripled.

I had gone to many conventions on evangelism, and I put everything I knew into practice in my congregation. We were proud to have a graduate of an American college as our minister of education; our Sunday school was tops. The youth organization was going well; so were the Boy Scouts, the Girl Scouts, the men's fellowship, and every other department.

Our follow-up system was one of the best. We had form letters number one, two, three, and four for every category—males, females, children, Jews, Arabs, anyone you could imagine. We had records of each telephone call and visit; we were pushing subscriptions to helpful magazines. The cards showed exactly how each person was doing, whether he had been baptized, everything.

The denomination was so impressed that I was invited to be a main speaker at two different conventions to share my follow-up system and distribute samples of all our forms to the pastors.

Yet underneath it all, I sensed that something wasn't right. Things seemed to stay high so long as I worked sixteen hours a day. But when I relaxed, everything came down. That disturbed me.

Finally, I decided to stop. I told my board, "I must go away for two weeks to pray." I headed for the countryside and gave myself to meditation and prayer.

The Holy Spirit began to break me down. The first thing He said was, "Juan, that thing you have is not a church. It's a business."

I didn't understand what He meant.

"You are promoting the gospel the same way Coca-Cola sells Coke," He said, "the same way Reader's Digest sells books and magazines. You are using all the human tricks you learned in school. But where is My finger in all of this?"

I didn't know what to say. I had to admit that my congregation was more of a business enterprise than a spiritual body.

Then the Lord told me a second thing. "You are not growing," He said. "You think you are, because you've gone from 200 to 600. But you're not growing—you're just getting fat."

What did that mean?

"All you have is more people of the same quality as before. No one is maturing; the level remains the same. Before, you had 200 spiritual babies; now you have 600 spiritual babies."

It was true. I couldn't deny a word of it.

"As a result," the Lord went on, "what you have is an orphanage instead of a church. Nobody has a father, spiritually speaking. You are not their father—you are the busy director of the orphanage. You're keeping the lights on and the bills paid and the bottles filled with milk, but neither you nor anyone else is actually parenting those babies."

Again, He was right.

When I got back home, I began to notice many evidences of permanent childhood—not only in my own congregation but throughout the Body of Christ.

For one example, prayers never seem to change. You would think that if a person were growing in his relationship with his Lord, he would say different things now from when he was first saved. But it isn't so.

Suppose I still spoke to my wife as I did when we first met. I remember that day. She was a member of my congregation, and I finally said to her, "Sister Martha, I'd like to say a few words to you, if we could be alone."

She answered, "Fine, pastor. Where shall we go?"

When we were alone I said, "Sister Martha, I don't know if you've noticed or not that I feel something different for you from the other sisters of the congregation . . . ."

Suppose that now—after more than twelve years of marriage and four children—I would come home and say, "Sister Martha, I'd like to say a few words to you . . . I don't know if you've noticed or not that I feel something different for you from the other sisters of the congregation . . . ." Hardly! We have grown in dialogue far beyond that early stage.

Yet in church, our people pray the same prayers and sing the same hymns they've always sung, The dialogue never escalates.

Another evidence is the division in the church. Paul told the Corinthians that their clinging to Peter, Apollos, and himself was a sign of spiritual babyhood. The Corinthians weren't fighting each other. They were just fond of different preachers. At least they stayed in the same congregation.

In our century we don't even do that well. We belong to different groups and meet in different buildings and speak against each other. If the Corinthians were babes in Christ, we haven't even been born yet.

And instead of getting better, we're getting worse. There are more denominations every year. The Body of Christ has never been so split.

A third evidence is that we are always interested in getting rather than giving. We are just like little children, constantly wanting the Lord to help us, do this for us, give us that, make us well, make us happy, give us money . . . we never stop begging. "Daddy, give me a dollar—please give me this, give me that."

The mature person knows how to give. Giving is one of the marks of an adult.

Isn't it interesting how Christians are always more intrigued with the gifts of the Spirit than with the fruit of the Spirit? If someone with a healing ministry comes along, the church is never so packed. Children love the spectacular. But only the mature are interested in love, joy, peace, patience, kindness, goodness, faithfulness, gentleness, and self-control.

Like children, we do not know how to value things. If you offer a child a hundred-dollar bill and a candy bar, he will take the candy bar every time. We are the same way when it comes to materialism. We always go for the nice home, the new car, the bank account rather than spiritual things, because we don't have a mature value system.

We even try to use God to get material things. It's not enough to seek after prosperity ourselves; we try to coax God into helping us get it! We are selfish children.

Another evidence: the lack of workers in the church. I don't understand it, but we have people who have been Christians for ten or twenty years and still can't lead a person to Christ. Their grand achievement is to invite someone to a meeting. "Why don't you come to our church? We have a nice building, nice carpeting, soft seats, it's all air-conditioned, and the pastor is a nice fellow—why don't you come along?"

If the person agrees, the Christian thinks he's done his duty. "Pastor, I brought my friend to the meeting. Now it's up to you from here on." So the pastor must preach the gospel, lead the person to Christ, baptize him, and care for him from then on.

Isn't it interesting how Paul baptized almost nobody? He told the Corinthians, "I thank God that I baptized none of you, except Crispus and Gaius . . . also the household of Stephanas; beyond that, I do not know whether I baptized any other" (1 Corinthians 1:14-16).

How is it, then, that Acts 18:8 says, "And Crispus, the leader of the synagogue, believed in the Lord with all his household, and many of the Corinthians, when they heard—, were believing and being baptized"? *Somebody* was baptizing the new believers, and it wasn't Paul. It must have been Crispus, Gaius, and other spiritual fathers who right away began caring for their spiritual children.

Every Sunday we preach the ABCs of salvation. People respond, and we put them in newcomers' classes to learn about the church, baptism, and the other fundamentals. But who takes them on from that point? By the time they finish our class, we're off to start another newcomers' class, leaving them with no guide to maturity.

No wonder we lose so many. No wonder the results of our big campaigns seem to shrink. The new believers—to put it plainly—get bored with church. Every Sunday is the same thing, the same songs by the same choir, the same preaching. Satan finds it very easy to pull them back into the kingdom of darkness.

Whose fault is this? The people are often told that they must grow. But how can they if they are never fed anything but milk? Milk is good for a while, but soon the baby needs something else.

The pastors, however, cannot be blamed entirely, for the seminaries and Bible colleges often have not prepared them. If all they know how to do is warm up milk, who is guilty then?

We are all victims of the structure in which we have been brought up. We cannot flee from the structure; it is woven into us. But we *can* make ourselves stop and think what we are doing. If we don't stop our ceaseless round of activities and ask God whether He is in it or not, then we are guilty after all.

It was very hard for me to stop. My phone was ringing from morning to night. I had to constantly keep oiling the machinery of my church—a machine I had put together in the first place—or else it would fall apart. In Argentina, pastors are even busier than usual because we often have one of the few cars in the congregation. So we are everyone's chauffeur; we take the sick people to the hospital and so forth, in addition to our other duties.

But praise the Lord, I finally stopped. And it brought a revolution to my congregation.

For the first time I wasn't laying out my human program and then saying, "Lord, please bless what I've planned." Instead I was saying, "Lord, what do You want me to do?"

It's incredible how many plans we pastors start and how few we finish. I've been to churches and heard pastors say, "Next month we are launching this program. Everything is all laid out and ready to roll."

The next year I see the pastor again and ask him, "How was that program, brother?"

"Oh, we couldn't do that," he explains. "But next week we have another thing beginning . . . ."

Why do our programs keep falling apart? Because we try to implement them by using children. And you cannot depend on children. They make great promises ("I'll do it—I'll behave properly—I *promise* I will"), but they don't follow through.

The Lord had to convince me that part of the problem was my preaching of nothing but milk. I thought I had really been doing well. But everything had been what the writer to the Hebrews called "elementary teaching."

Repentance.

Faith.

Washings (baptism).

The laying on of hands (the baptism in the Holy Spirit, which in the primitive church came usually right after water baptism when hands were laid on the person while he was still in the water).

The resurrection.

Eternal judgment.

That was all I'd preached in twenty years!

I looked at our Sunday school materials, and they covered these same foundation principles over and over again.

I went back to what I had received in Bible college—the same things. (You don't believe me? Look at the table of contents in any book of theology. You will find a chapter on the holy Scripture, a chapter on God, then man, then salvation, then the Holy Spirit, then the Second Coming and the last things. That's all. Nothing beyond "the first principles of the oracles of God," as the King James Version puts it.)

I belonged to a denomination that was proud of preaching four things: salvation, baptism in the Holy Spirit, healing, and the Second Coming. We called this the "Full Gospel"! Other groups have holiness as number two instead of the baptism in the Spirit.

How can this be the full gospel when Hebrews says it's *elementary?*

I don't mean to be critical of others; I was as guilty as anyone. I was dismayed to find that all these things—repentance, faith, water baptism, Spirit baptism, and preparation for the end times—were all completed the first day a person was saved in the early church! This was the starting line from which they went *on* to maturity.

Not long ago a pastor from another denomination said to me, "Oh, Pastor Ortiz, I'm really getting into deep water. I'm into a new dimension of the gospel I never knew was possible."

"What happened, brother?" I asked.

"Brother, I'm speaking in tongues now!" he said.

I said, "That's nothing. In the primitive church they spoke in tongues the first day they were saved. You think you've hit the climax of your life. You're still on the first principles—like most of the rest of us."

It really hit me hard when a boy in my congregation came to me and said, "Brother Juan, you know something? I'm just realizing that from the time I was saved a year ago, I learned and learned and learned in the church for about six months. But since then, it seems like I know everything everybody else knows. I'm just maintaining myself; I'm not growing like I used to."

Why wasn't his pastor giving him something besides milk?

I began trying to understand what solid food might be. I found Paul telling the Corinthians that he couldn't give them solid food since they were still babes needing milk. What did he talk about in 1 Corinthians? Immorality in the church, strife among brethren, marriage problems, food sacrificed to idols, insubordination, women's dress, abuses of the Lord's Supper, spiritual gifts, the resurrection of the dead, and how to take an offering.

Nothing but milk, Paul said.

He did give us a little peek at solid food in chapter 2:

> Yet we do speak wisdom among those who are mature; a wisdom, however, not of this age, nor of the rulers of this age, who are passing away;
> but we speak God's wisdom in a mystery, the hidden wisdom, which God predestined before the ages to our glory;
> the wisdom which none of the rulers of this age has understood; for if they had understood it, they would not have crucified the Lord of glory;
> but just as it is written,
> "Things which eye has not seen and ear has not heard,
> And which have not entered the heart of man,
> All that God has prepared for those who love Him."
> For to us God revealed them through the Spirit; for the Spirit searches all things, even the depths of God.
> For who among men knows the thoughts of a man except the spirit of the man, which is in him? Even so the thoughts of God no one knows except the Spirit of God.
> Now we have received, not the spirit of the world, but the Spirit who is from God, that we might know the things freely given us by God,
> which things we also speak, not in words taught by human wisdom, but in those taught by the Spirit, combining spiritual thoughts with spiritual words.
> But a natural man does not accept the things of the Spirit of God; for they are foolishness to him, and he cannot

understand them, because they are spiritually appraised.
   But he who is spiritual appraises all things, yet he himself is appraised by no man.
   For who has known the mind of the Lord, that he should instruct Him? But we have the mind of Christ.
                                                    —1 Corinthians 2:6-16

The very next verse (3:1) goes back to addressing "babes in Christ." What is Paul talking about in chapter 2?

He tells in another place about his personal trip to the central offices of the universe where he "heard inexpressible words, which a man is not permitted to speak" (2 Corinthians 12:4). Who knows what God shared with Paul then? He never included it in the New Testament.

The epistles, we must remember, are corrections. We don't have the mainstream of the apostolic teaching—only the corrections. We don't know all that Paul taught while he was actually in Corinth, Antioch, Troas, Thessalonica, and the other cities.

What is Romans about? Repentance. Hebrews, it clearly says in the passage I cited back at the beginning of this chapter, is scaled down so it won't choke the babes. (In our seminaries, Romans and Hebrews are "deep" epistles reserved for the third year of study!)

It is not too encouraging to realize that we haven't even drunk some of the milk available to us, and we haven't fully digested all the milk we've drunk. What will we do with "the wisdom not of this age"?

12

Growing Up

*And He gave some as apostles, and some as prophets, and
some as pastors and teachers,
    for the equipping of the saints for the work of service, to
the building up of the body of Christ:
    until we all attain to the unity of the faith, and of the
knowledge of the Son of God, to a mature man, to the measure
of the stature which belongs to the fulness of Christ.*
                                                —*Ephesians 4:11-13*

When the Lord began to speak to me about solutions to our
growth problem, He started with the passage in Ephesians.

My job was to equip the saints, to bring them to maturity.
I hadn't been taught that. I had been taught how to entertain
people, not how to perfect them. That was the idea of the
many activities of the church—to entertain, to maintain, to
keep people involved.

How many pastors have said to me almost as soon as I've come to their church, "Brother Ortiz, what new ideas do you have? Do you have any new ideas for the men's fellowship? Any new ideas for the young people?" We're always on the lookout for new, catchy ideas so we can maintain our people. If we can keep them in the grace of God until they die, we have succeeded, we think.

That is *not* our ministry as pastors. No wonder the apostle told the Hebrews, "Though by this time you ought to be teachers, you have need again for some one to teach you the elementary principles" (5:12). He must have been expecting something much better—that the laymen would eventually become teachers.

Ephesians 4 does not say that the apostles and prophets and pastors are to do the work of service. It says they are to equip the saints to do that. An architect does not build buildings; he plans how others should do it. If the architect also had to lay the brick and put the building together, he probably couldn't do more than one building in his entire lifetime. As it is, he can "build" several at once.

We need the apostolic ministry in the church today. We need leaders who can draw up God's blueprints and equip the believers to put the building together.

In addition, architects train other architects. Or, to go back to the Bible language, ministers bring forth ministers. Sheep bring forth lambs. Why shouldn't the sheep provide the milk for their own lambs? This is the natural way. It is also the key to multiplication.

The overall goal, says Paul, is to "attain . . . to the measure of the stature which belongs to the fulness of Christ." The Father wants everyone to grow up as tall as Jesus. Pastors must begin by reaching for maturity themselves first; then they will be ready to bring about the same growth in their sheep.

"As a result," Paul goes on in verses 14-15, "we are no longer to be children, tossed here and there by waves . . . but speaking the truth in love, we are to grow up in all aspects into Him, who is the head, even Christ."

The progression is like school. When we have come into first grade, we can teach others all about kindergarten. A year later, we should all have progressed so that we are in second grade, and are teaching others about first grade, and the first graders are teaching others about kindergarten. We are no longer teaching the ABCs of the gospel—but that does not mean they have been forgotten. They are still being taught, but by others at lower levels. The growth continues.

How could Paul have been willing to leave this world if he hadn't made disciples of Timothy, Philemon, Epaphras, and the others? Jesus went to heaven tranquil and satisfied because He was leaving behind twelve replicas of Himself. The twelve members of His congregation didn't have to write to any bishop and say, "Please send us another pastor because ours just left for heaven." They had grown up; they were ready to step into His shoes.

Why is it in the modern church that when someone wants to be trained for the ministry, he must *leave* the church and go to a seminary? The church is not fulfilling its job. If pastors were equipping the saints to do the work of service like the Bible says, the seminaries wouldn't be needed. God has only one agency on this earth: the Church. That's all He intended.

I had better explain: I'm not against seminaries and Bible schools and the other extrachurch organizations. The Church is weak; it needs crutches. In fact, praise the Lord for the crutches! But we should not spend our time building a crutch factory; we should instead look for the healing of the Church.

At the moment, we must be careful not to take crutches away from weak people. There's no reason to oppose the seminaries, the youth organizations, and the others; they are helping to hold us up. But when we are healed, the crutches will drop away. Let us pray toward that healing.

How will healing come about? The church will be able to grow up in Christ as it sees its leadership really take hold. Paul explains a progression in 1 Corinthians 12:28: "God has appointed in the church, first apostles, second prophets, third teachers, then miracles, then gifts of healings, helps, administrations, various kinds of tongues."

I never paid attention to the "first ... second ... third ... then ... then" before I began thinking about growing. In fact, I thought my ministry was quite mature because it included healing, administration, and tongues. I didn't see that all these things were on the lowest rung of the ladder.

But when I went alone to seek the Lord, He began to show me that this verse was a pyramid. The apostle was a man who also prophesied, taught, worked miracles and healings, helped, administrated, and spoke in tongues.

Again I saw that tongues were not the diploma at the end but rather one of the early lessons. Again I saw that if my church now had 600 tongues-speakers instead of 200 tongues-speakers, we hadn't grown. We had only become fatter.

I began to see why the family of God was not running smoothly. In most families, the first child is two or three years old when the second child comes along. When the third child comes, the second is a toddler and the first is almost ready for school.

But in the church, when the second child comes along, the first child is still a baby. The more children born into the church, the more diapers we have to change all at once.

But if everyone is growing, ministers and sheep alike, there is harmony. Look at Paul. He was not an apostle from the beginning. He was just a disciple who witnessed in the churches. He apparently first spoke in tongues when Ananias laid his hands on him (Acts 9). He kept growing. By Acts 11 and 12 he was a helper to Barnabas. Then came healing and miracles, and in Acts 13:1 he is listed among the prophets and teachers in Antioch.

Then he was sent out as an apostle.

Every Christian's ministry develops along this channel. But do you know what happens in the modern church? We pastors stop somewhere along the way; we know how to speak in tongues, to administrate, to help, to have some healings, or even to teach—but then we stop moving. We become corks. The sheep grow and grow and start jamming up behind us, unable to grow further until we grow some more ourselves. They keep listening to our sermons, and soon they know everything we know, and then we have nothing but a pressure chamber.

The pastor is not a cork intentionally; as I said before, he is a victim of the structure like everyone else. It's always been done that way.

If the pressure becomes great enough, the pastor gets uncomfortable enough to ask the bishop for a transfer. So the bishop takes out one cork and replaces him with another!

If it is a congregational denomination that doesn't have bishops, the problem is even worse. The pressure keeps building until the channel finally explodes and the cork flies out! He gets really banged up in the explosion, of course, sometimes so badly that he can no longer continue in the ministry.

All this is avoided, of course, if the pastor keeps on growing to apostleship and the sheep keep growing right behind him.

If a pastor is truly a father to his congregation, he cannot be changed (or exploded) every two or three years. What family changes fathers every two years? Maybe our churches are more like clubs that elect presidents for a certain term and then elect someone else. But if we are a family, we are a family, we stay together. The father keeps turning over responsibility to his sons as they grow.

Eventually, the minister is ready to be sent out as an apostle, which is what happened to Paul and Barnabas in Acts 13. They had become master builders of the church; they had been through all the stages. Now they were ready to plant new churches.

While in North America I often got letters from my disciples in Buenos Aires, saying, "Oh, how we wept when you left. We weep every time you go. But after you are gone, we understand how much we need to be alone." Four years ago some of them couldn't even say "Amen" by themselves, but now they are the pastors of the church. I can travel six, seven, or even eight months of the year because they are there in my place. If I would stay home, they wouldn't develop. They won't preach or lead the worship when I'm there—I'm a cork! But when I'm gone, they have to.

Even Jesus left His congregation—He finally left the earth altogether so His disciples would have to be alone and grow.

In the modern upside-down church, who is sent out to plant new churches? The young men fresh out of seminary! I started when I was only twenty years old. I didn't know what I was doing. What I planted wasn't a growing orchard—it was just a fruit stand on the corner. It had to be supplied continually from the outside. It couldn't produce any life of its own. Every time I had to be gone I had to call another pastor and say, "Please come and preach in my fruit stand because I'm going out."

Paul and Barnabas, being master builders, were equipped to plant growing, living orchards. They stayed a few months in each place and then moved on. After a couple of years, Paul said, "Let us return and visit the brethren in every city in which we proclaimed the word of the Lord, and see how they are" (Acts 15:36). They went back—and the orchards were still there and growing.

After Paul had been in Thessalonica, he wrote back to say, "Not only in Macedonia and Achaia, but also in every place your faith toward God has gone forth, so that we have no need to say anything. For they themselves report about us what kind of a reception we had with you" (1 Thessalonians 1:8-9).

It's obvious, isn't it, why back in Antioch the Holy Spirit did not say, "Set apart for Me Barnabas and Saul"—two of the principal ministers—"for the work to which I have called them" (Acts 13:2).

Today we are all upside down. The successful pastor is the one who stays in one place every Sunday of the year for the longest number of years. In the primitive church, the successful pastor was the one who could cause his disciples to grow faster and better and thus free himself to move on to a new task. Not because he was ousted, but because he could now leave that church in the hands of his sons and get out to other regions. He could always come home, as Paul came home to Antioch.

Today our missionaries are not like this. The most advanced pastors are the ones who stay home in America, we think. As a result, the missionaries are not really apostles (the two words come from the same root in Greek). They are just pastors. First they are pastors in America, and then they fly to Argentina and are pastors there. Does the airplane turn them into missionaries?

That is a very expensive thing for you North Americans, because an Argentine pastor can do the same job for only $200 a month. What makes a person a true apostle, a missionary? His experience and the gift of God within him which enables him to plan the strategy for a whole region, to train workers, to plant living orchards everywhere.

We must all grow up. We must leave our permanent childhood and absorb solid food until we are equipped ourselves and are equipping others to spread the Kingdom of God.

13

Members or Disciples?

You also, as living stones, are being built up as a spiritual house for a holy priesthood.

—*1 Peter 2:5*

If only Peter's statement were true today! In some places it is, but more often the church is not a spiritual house—it is a pile of loose bricks. There is a big difference.

Each member of the congregation is a brick, and we all work very hard to accumulate more and more bricks. Even the pastor works in evangelism, trying to bring more bricks to our construction site.

But there is a problem with loose bricks: They can be stolen. The pastor and his people must be always on guard that someone from another church doesn't come along and steal bricks for *their* lot. In fact, we are all so busy watching and hoarding that the building never gets built.

We are God's bricks. But we have not been put into place in His building where we can support some weight and give strength. If we were, we would know which bricks are under us, which are above us, and how we relate to each other. But as it is, we spend all our time checking on each other. We are so afraid that someone is going to slip away. Meanwhile, we forget all about the unsaved people who are out in the cold looking for a warm building to take them in.

If the pastor tries to pick us up and put us in place in the building, we resist. The church must be run democratically, we say. We don't submit to any one person. We submit only to the majority vote (and sometimes not even then). I've heard Christians say very proudly, "I don't follow any man—I follow Christ." That sounds pious, but its really a great mistake. It means the person wants to do his own will; he doesn't even realize what it means to follow Christ.

Paul said, "Be imitators of me, just as I also am of Christ" (1 Corinthians 11:1). We pastors are sometimes afraid to say that because we are not living as we should. We say instead, "Don't look at me, brother—just follow the Bible."

You know what that means? It means, "I tried it, and I couldn't make it work—*you* try it!" No wonder the layman is discouraged. If the pastor can't do what the Bible says, who can?

Paul was not afraid to be a model. He told the Philippians, "The things you have learned and received and heard and seen in me, practice these things; and the God of peace shall be with you" (4:9). That's not very democratic, but it leads to the construction of a strong building.

The reason it works is based in the multiplication element. Once an old woman in Argentina introduced me to a girl. "This is my granddaughter," she said.

"Is that so?" I replied.

"Yes, I have great-grandchildren," she said. "One of them is fifteen already, so if she marries soon I may even have great-great-grandchildren."

"How many children did you have?" I asked.

"Six."

"And now you have how many grandchildren?"

"Thirty-six."

"And how many great-grandchildren?"

"Who knows?" she said. "I've never counted them."

According to that proportion, she could have 216 great-grandchildren and 1,296 great-great-grandchildren!

Her family was quite impressive, too; one son was a doctor, another a lawyer, two were farmers, one was a taxi driver. Among her grandsons were engineers and many other professional people.

If I had asked her, "How did you manage such a large family—all these well-fed, well-dressed, well-educated people?" she would have replied, "I didn't. I just took care of the six."

And each of them took care of their own six.

We have no such multiplication system in the church. The poor pastor has to take care of everybody, and that is the problem.

In order to grow and expand and build the bricks into a building, we must do something about that. We must make disciples out of people so they can make disciples of more people. We must be fathers, not orphanage directors.

Even Jesus did it this way. Wasn't He the best pastor who ever lived? Yet He took care of only twelve. Matthew 9:36 says, "And seeing the multitudes, He felt compassion for them, because they were distressed and downcast like sheep without a shepherd."

Why? Wasn't He the Good Shepherd? Yes, He was. But a shepherd cannot take care of an unlimited number of sheep—not even Jesus. If He couldn't make more than twelve disciples at a time, how can I?

Jesus placed them in the building very well. When He left, they knew what to do: Go and make disciples of others just as Jesus had done with them.

So they went and began teaching and sharing from house to house in small units. We don't do that anymore in the modern church. We get everybody together on Sundays in the orphanage dining hall and say, "All right—everybody open your mouth! Here comes the food." We sling it out en masse and then say, "Good-by. You are dismissed until next week."

That's no way to feed children. We must take each one in our arms, one by one, and put the bottle in his mouth. As he grows he will be able to handle it more for himself, and eventually he will be able to help us prepare food for the younger ones—he has a growing place in the family.

This is the ministry of edifying, building up—not caretaking.

Of course, we must ask ourselves what it is we are edifying. A denomination? I found myself doing that for a long time. At the conventions I took great pride in what my group was building; it was another little kingdom.

Then I realized that Paul told us to work toward "the building up of the body of Christ" (Ephesians 4:12). We don't understand that today. We don't think in terms of the whole Body of Christ. We think in terms of the Baptist segment of the Body of Christ, or the Presbyterian segment, or the Assemblies of God segment. We like to pretend that the part is the whole thing.

Paul told the Corinthians that it was a very serious thing not to "judge the body rightly" (1 Corinthians 11:29), or as the King James Version puts it, "not discerning the Lord's body." The one bread of the Lord's Supper means that even though we are many, we are one.

How can we build something we don't understand? We can't. And we aren't. We are building instead our own kingdoms, denominations, and programs at the expense of other parts of the Body.

103

We are crazy! If you see a man cutting his foot with a knife, you will say, "What in the world are you doing?"

"I'm cutting my foot!"

"Why?"

"Because this foot stepped on the other one, and it said, 'Cut him!' "

The man is out of his mind. He doesn't have the discernment to realize that both feet belong to the same body.

Sometimes when you are eating, your teeth bite your tongue. Aaaugh! But you don't decide to pull out all your teeth because of that. Your tongue, even though it has the power of speech, doesn't say, "Let's get rid of the teeth." It is understood that the teeth belong to the body.

Listen: We must understand what the Body of Christ is. We must stop doing crazy things to ourselves, speaking against each other—no wonder we hurt. No wonder the church is weak and bleeding.

The people who killed the physical body of Christ—Pontius Pilate, the Roman executioners, the Jewish priests—at least they had a purpose. It was a terrible thing to do, but at least it resulted in Jesus paying for our sins.

But what is our purpose when we persecute the spiritual Body of Christ? What is our reason for crucifying and hurting and dividing this Body? We have none, and our punishment for doing so will be even greater than Pilate's or Judas'.

Maybe the Lord's Supper can teach us to love and respect and build up the Body—the *whole* Body. If we don't learn this, we are crazy.

The whole Body must, as the Americans say, "get it together." The arms and legs and ears must be solidly connected to each other. "For just as we have many members in one body and all the members do not have the same function," says Romans 12:4-5, "so we, who are many, are one body in Christ, and individually members one of another."

I have already written about Ephesians 4:11-15. Verse 16 speaks of Christ, "from whom the whole body, being fitted and held together by that which every joint supplies, according to the proper working of each individual part, causes the growth of the body for the building up of itself in love."

Let me make this very strong: If the members are not "fitted and held together," they're not a body. They're an assortment of limbs.

What is a church member today? Nearly every local church has three requirements:

(1) The person must attend the meetings.

(2) The person must give his money.

(3) The person must live a life of good character.

If he does those three, he is considered a good church member. He's like a good club member; he attends the club, pays his dues, and tries not to embarrass the club.

But when we in Buenos Aires started looking for this in the Gospels and the Acts of the Apostles, we couldn't find it. In fact, we couldn't find the word *member* anywhere. In all the accounts of the primitive church, we couldn't find where they took members into the church or made a special ceremony or anything.

But in reading Acts, we found another word that really revolutionized our lives and our church—the word *disciple*. We asked ourselves, "What is a disciple?"

It wasn't anything like a church member. A disciple is a person who learns to live the life his teacher lives. And gradually he teaches others to live the life he lives.

So discipleship is not a communication of knowledge or information. It is a communication of *life*. That's why Jesus said, "The words that I have spoken to you are spirit and are life" (John 6:63).

Discipleship is more than getting to know what the teacher knows. It is getting to be what he is.

That's why the Bible says we are to *make* disciples. That

is much more than just *talking* to them, or *winning* them, or *instructing* them. The *making* of a disciple means the creating of a duplicate.

Obviously, then, the teacher must be a disciple himself. In the ordinary type of teaching, you can fight with your wife over the breakfast table and then go to the church and preach about love in the home. But when making disciples, you cannot do that. Your disciples are with you much more; they get into your home, they see how you live, and that is what they imitate.

Suppose someone were traveling with me for a week and would say, "Listen, Juan Carlos, you are a teacher—please take some time and teach me something." I would answer, "If you have learned nothing by being with me the last seven days, I have nothing to teach you now." Discipleship is not so much talk as it is living.

We must think about three dimensions of teaching: revelation, formation, and information.

Revelation is something that only God can do. If I were to describe Rio de Janeiro to you, the atmosphere of the city, Guanabara Bay, Sugar Loaf Mountain, the beaches—you still could not say that you know Rio de Janeiro. You know something about it, but you will never know it until you go there and the city is revealed to you.

In the same way God must reveal Himself to us face to face before we can say that we know Him.

Actually, my description of Rio would be the minimum dimension of teaching: information. It is the way we used to teach in our Sunday school and church.

Q—How many books does the Bible have?

A—Sixty-six.

Q—Which is the Psalm of the Good Shepherd?

A—Psalm 23.

And so forth. We were informed about Abraham and

Moses, heaven and hell, angels and demons, the fall of
Satan, the church, the Second Coming. Information is not
bad, but it's the least way of teaching. All it does is possibly
awaken your interest to experience the things you are informed about.

Unfortunately, we made this an end in itself. To know
and memorize the words of the Bible was our only goal.

The strange thing is that Jesus almost never used this
method. We never see Jesus giving His disciples a Bible
study. Can you imagine Him saying, "Well, don't forget that
tomorrow morning we'll be having devotions from eight to
nine. From nine to ten we'll have minor prophets. Then from
ten to eleven we will have the poetry books, and then from
eleven to noon we will have homiletics and hermeneutics."

Yet He was preparing the best ministers history ever
saw. How could He forget such important subjects?

Can you hear Him saying, "Now we are going to study
the book of Jeremiah. According to higher criticism,
Jeremiah is a mythical figure; he never actually existed. Or if
he existed, he was not the author of this book . . . ."

Never! Jesus had no time to lose. He was simple, clear,
and concrete. Many of our Bible studies try to be the same,
but we only end up making things more confused.

Once I was asked to teach a class in the Argentine Bible
School on the book of Romans. Since Romans is so important, it should be taught verse by verse, I thought. So I
did. It took me an entire year to get through. By the time we
finished, I don't think anyone knew what Romans was trying to say.

Suppose you get a letter from me which reads, "Dear Bill:
I'm writing to you from Rome, where I have just arrived with
my wife and children. So far we have seen . . ." and I go on
with a long letter.

You go to church the next Sunday and you say, "Friends,
we have received a letter from Brother Juan Carlos. Over the
next three months now, we will study it.

"He begins his letter by saying, 'Dear Bill.' Now in the Greek the word *dear* means a person who is loved. He refers to me as a loved one. I can imagine Brother Juan taking his pen and writing *dear*. His heart is overflowing with love. His wife beside him joins in his love.

"Brothers and sisters, how do you write your letters? Do you begin them with the word *dear?* Let us all begin doing that from now on.

" 'Dear Bill'—he calls me by my name. He knows me. He is concerned for me as a person. How about you? Do you call people by name and let them know that you recognize them?

" 'I'm writing to you . . . .' He writes to us himself! He isn't using a secretary; he writes to us directly.

"Well, that's all for today. Next week we will continue in the letter from Juan Carlos."

The next Sunday: " 'I'm writing to you from Rome.' Ah, the city founded by Romulus and Remus, who were fed by the wolves. The capital city of the Roman Empire, where the Caesars lived. You will remember that the empire eventually split into two parts, the eastern and the western, and then collapsed.

"Now we will go to the next verse . . . ."

And the people of the congregation say, "Our pastor is so deep! My, he can go two or three weeks on one verse—tremendous!"

At the end of three months, you will have finished my letter, but no one will know what I said.

Yet that's how we teach the Bible. It's going to be interesting when we get to heaven and Paul grabs some of us teachers and says, "Come here—I want to talk to you. I *never* wrote what you said I did!"

We like to impress people by the amount of information we know about a Bible text. We think we are being "deep." But does anyone really understand what we're saying? I doubt it.

We are concerned with *information*. But Jesus was concerned with *formation*. We need to learn from Him how to form disciples.

14

Formation of Disciples

"God to the lost sheep of the house of Israel.
"And as you go, preach, saying, "The kingdom of heaven
is at hand,'
"Heal the sick, raise the dead, cleanse the lepers, cast out
demons; freely you received, freely give . . . .
"And into whatever city or village you enter, inquire who
is worthy in it; and abide there until you go away.
"And as you enter the house, give it your greeting."
—Matthew 10:6-8, 11-12

Jesus had the pattern for forming disciples. He gave His own
disciples concrete things to *do* instead of things to store away
in their brains. And they obeyed Him.

He didn't preach inspirational sermons to motivate
them. He didn't have to. Inspirational sermons are for
disobedient people who need to be coaxed. They need their
emotions played upon so they can sense how nice it would be

110

if maybe they would do what Jesus commanded!

If we were under the lordship of Christ, He could just say the word, and we wouldn't need any soft organ music or soothing words from the pulpit—we would do as we were told. Jesus didn't say to His twelve, "How would you like to go? Maybe you could take a nice little trip around the area now?" No. He commanded, and they did it. That is how disciples are formed.

In order to form lives, we must stop being speakers and start being fathers. Speakers have only hearers. Fathers have children. Learning doesn't come by hearing but by obeying.

What happens when we speakers get through? Our hearers say, "Thank you very much, pastor. That was a nice sermon." Is that all?

When the seventy came back to Jesus after obeying His commands, they told about the demons being submissive to them. Jesus didn't say, "Oh, thank you for doing what I said." Instead He had another command: "Do not rejoice in this...rejoice that your names are recorded in heaven" (Luke 10:20).

When James and John wanted to call down fire on the hostile Samaritans, the Bible specifically says, "He turned and rebuked them" (Luke 9:55). He was forming them.

When Peter objected to the idea of the crucifixion, Jesus said, "Get behind Me, Satan! You are a stumbling-block to Me" (Matthew 16:23). Can you imagine a modern pastor saying that to one of his flock?! Like it or not, rebuking is part of the formation process in discipleship.

Here is the first law of discipleship: *There is no formation without submission.* Club-type members don't submit. In fact, it's the other way around—they want the pastor to submit to them, because they hold the vote in the club. Again we are upside down. In the Gospel according to the Saint Evangelicals, the pastor submits to the membership. In the gospel of the Kingdom, the arm controls the fingers, not the other way around.

Submission is so obvious in the Bible. "Be subject to one another in the fear of Christ," says Ephesians 5:21. "Obey your leaders, and submit to them; for they keep watch over your souls, as those who will give an account" (Hebrews 13:17).

The only way I can form the lives of my four children is if they submit to me. Suppose each time I go to correct them, I run the risk of them running off to another father and saying, "I don't want to be the child of Juan Carlos Ortiz anymore—I want to be your child." And suppose that man would say, "Oh, welcome—come on in." I would have to stop correcting my children, because I don't want to lose them. I love them. But I *do* correct them, because I'm sure they are going to stay in my home no matter what. They are submitted.

In the church, the pastors cannot form lives because if he gets too hard with one of his children, the child will run off to another orphanage. Paul told Titus, "Speak and exhort and reprove with all authority. Let no one disregard you" (Titus 2:15). We pastors must first speak to our children. If they don't obey, then we must exhort. If nothing happens still, we must reprove with all authority. Otherwise we will have spoiled children.

Suppose we formed our own children by the church system. I would say to my family, "Come now—it's time for service. Today the sermon is going to be about washing your face and ears. Sit down now. First we're going to sing a nice chorus. It goes like this: 'Soap is a wonderful thing—wonderful, wonderful/And when it's mixed with water, it makes the bubbles flow, flow, flow.' Isn't it nice? Don't you love that chorus?

"Now for the message. Soap was invented in China about four centuries before Christ. It comes in bars of different sizes and colors and different perfumes. It is made of various minerals or vegetable or animal oils, according to the price. And when you mix it with water and apply it to your face and ears, it makes you nice and clean.

"Of course, if you get it into your eyes, it will burn. But even so, it won't burn very long, and if you're careful, you can avoid this altogether.

"So this is the way to keep your face and ears clean. Now while the organ plays softly and the choir sings, 'Just As I Am,' if any of you are touched deeply and you want to wash your face and ears, please raise your hand."

That is not the way to form lives. At least it's not the way my mother did it. She gave a command, and I obeyed; now I wash my own face and ears without her having to worry about it!

The second law of discipleship: *There is no submission without submission.* (You think I wrote a mistake there, but I didn't.) The person giving commandments to his disciples must be under the command of someone himself. He rebukes his disciples—who rebukes him? There is no submission if there is not submission at every level.

You remember the Roman centurion who asked Jesus to heal one of his servants. Jesus said, "I will come and heal him."

Then the centurion said, "Lord, I am not qualified for You to come under my roof, but just say the words, and my servant will be healed. For I too am a man under authority, with soldiers under me; and I say to this one, 'Go!' and he goes, and to another, 'Come!' and he comes, and to my slave, 'Do this!' and he does it" (Matthew 8:7-9).

He understood that to have authority means being under authority. I cannot create the authority for my own life. It must come from outside. Romans 13:1 says, "There is no authority except from God, and those which exist are established by God." What if God has installed two or three levels above me? Fine. Only when I am in line can authority pass through me to others.

Imagine a sergeant in the army. He tells a private to do something, and the private does it. The sergeant gets all excited and says to himself, *How powerful I am! I think I'll resign from the army and make my own army in my neighborhood.*

He goes back home to the old gang. "All right!" he says, "You guys do this!" They laugh at him.

What happened? He lost his authority when he rejected the authority over himself. Our trouble in the church is that we want to have authority and still be independent. That is impossible. You cannot be an independent and have authority. If you want the right to control others, you must be under the control of others yourself. It is an eternal law of God.

This is very important. Formation requires not only submission but intersubmission.

How did we implement these things in Buenos Aires? Well, the first thing was for me to come under the authority of the ministers of my city. (I will explain this later.) I was then eligible to begin making disciples in my own congregation.

We decided to stop using the word *member,* because it sounded too much like a club with no submission. We said we would use the word *disciple* instead. Everyone understood what a disciple was and knew that he was not there yet.

So if you had asked someone, "Are you a member of this church?" he would have said, "Yes, I'm member number 234—here's my credential."

But if you had asked, "Are you a disciple?" he would have said, "Oh, no. Not yet. I don't even know if the pastor is truly a disciple yet. He hasn't placed me under someone to be formed into a disciple."

I kept preaching discipleship for a year and a half without knowing how to get started. Everyone understood the concept, but we didn't know how to change. Finally in my frustration I said, "Look, Jesus chose twelve disciples and built from there. I am the Rev. Juan Carlos Ortiz and I have to keep serving my club, but I'm also going to start an underground church on the side."

So Johnny started in his own home. Johnny stole the deacons from the Rev. Juan Ortiz's club and began trying to make disciples of them. (In this new structure, I'm not a Reverend anymore; I'm just Johnny. Before, I had to be respected. Now all I want is to be loved.)

I gave my life to these disciples. I served them. We went out to the countryside together. We ate together; they slept in my home and I slept in theirs. We became a family.

After about six months or so (it didn't happen overnight), the whole club began to notice how my disciples were more interested in helping them, in loving them, in sharing and counseling. So I allowed my disciples to steal a few more members and begin making disciples of them themselves.

It took us almost three years, but we eventually changed the whole club into a discipleship family of more than 1500.

This meant, of course, that we had to set up a number of cells. During the changeover, new people were being saved in the cells, but we forbade them to come to the club-type church because we didn't want to spoil them with the old structure. Eventually, the old structure was finished. Praise the Lord.

You know what we did then? We staged a mock persecution. We pretended that our building had been taken away from us for a whole month. We met just in homes, and on Sundays we went to visit other congregations—Catholic, Baptist, whatever. Each of my five disciples had a group in a different part of the city. Cacho, for example—he's an auto body repairman who has 300 disciples in cells under him. He works nine hours a day in the body shop and still forms the lives of more people than a lot of full-time ministers. Cacho and his 300 went to a Baptist church of only about 100 people.

Can you imagine! In walk 300 visitors. "Where are all of you from?"

"We are from Brother Ortiz's congregation."

"Why are you here?"

"We just came to visit you."

"What about your meeting?"

"Well, we closed our meeting to come and be with you."

You see, with this structure you can do anything you want. You can pull the whole body together within a matter of hours if needed. The next time we have a mock persecution, we will do it in winter to see how it goes. Maybe some day we can do without a building altogether. But we won't sell it. We'll put in beds and dining rooms and use it to help the poor of the area. It will also be a center for visitors and traveling apostles.

But it will never again be a cave where believers hide from the world. Jesus never said, "Sinners, come to the church." He said, "Believers, go into the world and make disciples."

The church sits in the pews and sings, "Come home, come home/Ye who are weary, come home." We should sing instead, "Go ye, go ye/Ye who are seated, go ye." We have it all upside down. Sinners are dead, lost, deaf, blind. Yet we put up posters for the blind to read. If we can't mobilize the Christians who are supposed to be alive, how can we ever hope to mobilize the unsaved?

Our cells, on the other hand, are already in the world. They meet anywhere—a home, a park, a restaurant, on the beach. Some meet at six o'clock in the morning. Others meet at midnight because people work late. They are flexible.

Eventually we came back to use the word *member,* but with a whole new definition. A body-type member is:

(1) One who is dependent. You never see a nose walking along the street by itself. The body must be joined together as a body. If a member is independent, his is not part of the body.

(2) A part of the body that unites two other parts. The forearm unites the hand with the upper arm.

(3) One who passes along nourishment. He receives nourishment for himself and for the other members under him.

(4) One who sustains, who stays put. A member of the body can't be jerked out of the body. Does your wife ever say

116

when you come home, "Where did you lose your right leg?" Impossible. You don't lose your members.

(5) One who passes along orders. The head gives an order to the hand, but it must be passed through other members in between. The hand never gets disgusted with the forearm and says, "I think I'll detach myself from you and put in a cable from me directly to the head." No. We are a body.

(6) One who is elastic. Bodies are flexible. Organizations walk like robots. In the past, someone with a new idea or a new talent usually had to get out of the church in order to minister. People with vision had to go to Campus Crusade, to Youth for Christ, to the Navigators, or somewhere else to give expression to their vision.

But when the church is a body of disciples, it is flexible. The church is spread to all parts of the world; it is free to be the salt of the earth and the light of the world.

15

The Holy Protestant Traditions

"Who was I that I could stand in God's way?"
—Acts 11:17

I can still remember how proud I was the day my first son went off to school. All the schoolchildren in Argentina wear white overalls, and we had gone to the best store to buy the strongest, most expensive ones we could find. He looked so nice.

We weren't so happy, though, six months later when we found that the good quality overalls could no longer be worn. David had grown. We had to lay them aside and go buy a larger pair.

By now, of course, we know better. For each of our four children we buy the cheapest overalls in the store, because we know that in six months they won't fit anyway.

118

That is the way it works with any kind of structure. Structures serve us very well so long as everything stays the same. But when we grow, the structures don't fit anymore.

So it was in our church. The more we grew in discipleship, the more we found that our structures were hindering the new flow of the Spirit. Not because the structures were wrong. We did not despise them; we just acknowledged that they were made for yesterday instead of today.

Leaders must not get offended when we speak about changing structures. It means only that we are growing. If we can live for years and years with the same structures, it is proof that we are not growing. For example, we had used the same hymnal in my church for forty years. Since God began to renew us, we have changed the hymnal five times.

New wine calls for new wineskins. The difference is not in the style; it is not that one skin is more attractive or more in fashion than the other. Old wineskins are not discarded because they are old; they are discarded because they are *hard*. The skin must be flexible and elastic to accommodate the new wine.

The old wineskins which Jesus talked about in Matthew 9:17 are old traditional structures, which are often harder than anything else. Some of us could omit a verse of two of the Bible easier than omit one tradition! We often clash with the Bible in order to follow our structure.

Once I asked a Catholic, "Listen—where do you find the worship of Mary in the Bible?" I really wanted to straighten him out.

He was very humble. He said, "Well, it's possible that the Catholic Church does emphasize Mary too much, but at least there is a Mary in the Bible, isn't there?"

"Yes," I said.

"But where in the Bible are the denominations which you defend so much?" he wanted to know.

You see, our denominations are our traditions, regardless of what the Bible says. Jesus has only one wife, the Church. He is not a polygamist. Yet we tell people that in some mysterious way the denominations are even part of the will of God! We make God guilty for our divisions, our lack of love. And then we criticize the Catholics for their traditions.

At least their traditions are older than ours. We ought not to try to remove the specks from Catholic eyes until we get the logs out of our own. (I started at the beginning of this renewal to write a book entitled *The Holy Traditions of the Protestant Church*. But I realized that I wasn't writing it in love, so I quit.)

I have already mentioned our tradition of closing our eyes to pray. The Bible more than once illustrates exactly the opposite.

I have also noted how the Bible says, "He who has believed and has been baptized shall be saved" (Mark 16:16). Our tradition has decided that he who has believed and has been saved shall, after months of trial, be baptized.

Jesus told us to "Go therefore and make disciples of all the nations, baptizing them in the name of the Father and the Son and the Holy Spirit, teaching them to observe all that I commanded you" (Matthew 28:19-20). Our tradition says to go and make disciples, teaching them to observe all that Jesus commanded, and then baptize them. In some cases, the church members must even vote on the person before he can be baptized.

Where did we get this? I don't know. It's part of the holy Protestant tradition. And we will oust people from the church if they don't line up with the tradition in every respect.

Traditions and structures are so strong! Sometimes I almost wonder if they don't have an evil spirit behind them. It's amazing to see the power of tradition even in an apostle like Peter when he was sent to Cornelius.

Peter had been standing right there the day Jesus had said, "Go therefore and make disciples of all nations" (Matthew 28:19). He had also heard Jesus specifically command them to "be My witnesses both in Jerusalem, and in all Judea and Samaria, and even to the remotest part of the earth" (Acts 1:8).

But when it came right down to being a witness to Cornelius, a Gentile centurion, Peter's tradition wouldn't stretch. The Lord kept hitting him with the vision of the animals in the sheet and saying, "What God has cleansed, no longer consider unholy"—and Peter kept insisting, "By no means, Lord . . ." (Acts 10:14-15). Traditions have a mysterious power; sometimes they even overwhelm the words of God Himself.

It is tradition that makes us say, "Lord, NO!" We read in the Bible about the unity of the Body of Christ, and we say, "No! God wants the denominations the way they are." The Bible is the rule of faith and practice, we say—unless it conflicts with our tradition. Fantastic.

At last the Lord says to Peter, "Behold, three men are looking for you. But arise, go downstairs, and accompany them without misgivings; for I have sent them Myself" (verses 19-20). (He doesn't say the three men are Gentiles, or what their mission is.) Peter finally decides he can obey at least that much.

The men tell an amazing story of Cornelius praying, receiving an angelic visit, and being directed to Joppa to this exact street and house number to find a man by the name of Simon! What can the apostle say? He has to go along.

But he is bucking every step of the way. He walks into Cornelius' house, and almost the first thing he says is, "You know that it's an abomination for people like us to come see people like you" (that's a rough translation from the Spanish Bible).

What if somebody came to your house and said that? You'd say, "Look, sir, there's the door!"

You can imagine how Cornelius feels. He has invited all his friends and relatives to his home. "You're going to meet a real man of God," he's told them. "An angel told me to call him. He's such a holy, perfect man, and he'll explain to us all about God."

Then Peter walks in and insults him.

Peter comments on why he bothered to come at all, and then says, "So I ask for what reason you have sent for me" (verse 29).

An apostle of Jesus Christ—and he doesn't know what to do?! Even a small child would know. Peter knows he's asking a stupid question. But he is not willing to give the message. Why? Tradition.

So Cornelius tells his story all over again, repeating what his men told Peter two days before. And Peter finally begins to preach. He explains about Jesus, His miracles, His death and resurrection.

Is Peter willing to go ahead and call the Gentiles to repentance? I don't think so! I think he's stalling around . . . when God finally breaks through in spite of him and the people begin praising the Lord, speaking in tongues, weeping, perhaps dancing—who knows?

Peter dashes into the other room for a conference with his Jewish friends. "What's going on in there?" someone asks. "Peter, what did you do?"

"I didn't do anything!" Peter says. "I didn't baptize them in the Spirit—God did. I can't help it!"

"Well, what are we going to do now? Do we baptize them in water?"

The Gentiles have no problem—they're enjoying the outpouring of the Spirit. But the traditionalists have a tremendous problem. Their structure has been rattled.

They argue about it. Finally Peter says, "Well, I think we should baptize them. After all, if God—"

"Peter! What are you going to say to the executives back in Jerusalem?"

"I don't know, but I can't think of a reason not to baptize them."

When they get back to Jerusalem, the news has already beaten them. Peter walks in. "Hello, brother—how are you?" he says to someone.

"There's a board meeting at six o'clock."

"What?"

"You heard me—a board meeting at six o'clock."

"What for?"

"You'll find out when you get there."

The meeting opens. "All right, Peter," someone says, "we've heard that you went into a Gentile home and *ate* with them! Don't touch us, don't touch us! Now, is that true?"

Peter begins to tell the story. ". . . And as I began to speak, the Holy Spirit fell upon them—"

"No! No!"

"—Just as He did upon us at the beginning—"

"No!"

". . . If God therefore gave to them the same gift as He gave to us also after believing in the Lord Jesus Christ, who was I that I could stand in God's way?"

Listen to what the Bible says: "And when they heard this, they quieted down, and glorified God, saying, 'Well then . . .' " (Acts 11:15-18).

The power of tradition is awesome. God cannot do many things He would like to do because of our bondage. We are scandalized every time He wants us to change a little.

Our minds are like small end tables that can hold only a lamp or a few books. There is no use lowering a refrigerator onto the table because it would break. That's what happens when our traditional minds receive something more than we have been accustomed to. We fall apart.

I remember the first time I went to an Assembly of God church and saw people clapping their hands. "Ohhhhh!" I said. "These people are so worldly." I told them so. My mind just couldn't take it.

But then they reminded me of all the places in the

Psalms that speak of clapping the hands before the Lord.

The same thing happened the first time I saw people begin to dance before the Lord. Ohhhhh! I was scandalized. My tradition would not allow it. Again God let me know that He had cleansed such a thing, and I ought not to call it unclean.

Remember the woman who came and broke the perfume bottle over Jesus? The disciples were aghast. "What is the point of this waste?" they wanted to know (Matthew 26:8).

Jesus said, "She has done a good deed to Me" (verse 10). Tremendous! His mind was not upset in the least.

We must ask God to strengthen our tables so we can take whatever weight He wants to drop on us. He wants to do greater things in our time, but He holds back for fear of crushing us.

What must we do to experience the full will of God? Two things, says Romans 12:1-2. First, we must present our bodies as a living and holy sacrifice. A living sacrifice is better than a dead one, because a living sacrifice has a future. God can do whatever He wished with it.

Secondly, we must be transformed by the renewing of our minds. We must be *ready for change*. Being in the will of God means being continually open to change. Sometimes we say, "Lord, show me Your will," but it wouldn't make any difference to us if He did. We're like a train saying, "Please steer me down the track." What for? The tracks are already laid.

The tracks are our traditions. We pray, "Lord, help us to do Thy will," but the tracks are already nailed down.

We're like the children in the kiddie cars at the amusement park. They turn the wheel this way and that, but the car goes the same way every time regardless. That's how we are in the church and in the denominational councils. We make all kinds of motions, but everything stays the same.

16

Changing Traditions

> *Therefore I exhort the elders among you ... shepherd the flock of God among you, not under compulsion, but voluntarily, according to the will of God ....*
>
> *—1 Peter 5:1-2*

When God began to renew us, there were some traditions that had to be changed.

The tradition of democracy was one of the strongest traditions we had. We began to see that the primitive church was not very democratic. It was theocratic. God commanded the apostles, who told the people what he wanted. They also put elders in the churches. Everyone was obedient.

It was a church commanded by the head, not the feet. The power flowed from the top through the middle to the bottom.

In a democracy, things are the other way around. The power is in the base. The head must obey the orders of the feet.

There is no record of Paul saying, "Timothy, could I interest you in volunteering for the ministry? We'd really like to have you join us if you like."

Acts 16:3 says, "Paul wanted this man to go with him; and he took him . . . ." That's all there was to it.

The apostles even had the right to define doctrine. The New Testament speaks often not of "Jesus' doctrine" but of "the apostles' doctrine." They were infallible.

The problems arose when the theocratic church lost its charisma, its spiritual power. The leaders became more conscious of material, earthly power than what came from above. They kept the same form of government, but the spirit was gone. They were like a pen case without the pen inside. They looked the same externally, but on the inside they were empty.

The pope continued to think of himself as infallible, and I can understand why. After all, the letters Peter had written, the letters of John and the others, were all the truth. Why shouldn't that continue? It could have; but without the charisma, the divine revelation from heaven, the Church became a dangerous thing in the world.

Some of the sons of the Church—Savonarola, Huss, Luther, and others—tried to renew it, but the Church would not accept their ministries. They could have brought new life to the Catholic Church, but instead they were driven out. That is the problem of power without revelation.

So the Protestant churches reacted and decided to be democratic. That was good for a time; it brought the so-called laymen back into the work of the church. They had to think once again, to vote, to work.

But it was not the cure. In the Dark Ages the pope had become the substitute for the word of the Lord. Now the majority vote became the substitute. The people still didn't know

126

for sure what God was saying. Instead, they said, "Let's vote on it, and whatever gets more than half must be the will of God."

The majority is not always right, It was the majority who made the golden calf in the wilderness. It was the majority who turned away from Jesus after His teaching in John 6.

And in these days when God is restoring ministries and charismas, we are going to have a lot of trouble with democracy. I'm not arguing for an episcopal form of government, but neither can I support a democratic form of government. Without charisma, neither one is biblical. Perhaps when God brings renewal, people in episcopal forms are more receptive—I don't know. They are already used to taking orders from people without the fulness of the Spirit; what will they do if their bishops really are in touch with God?

The church government question has been discussed at length throughout history, and I don't think it can be solved for this reason: A biblical form of church government won't work in a nonbiblical church.

The Bible speaks of the church in only two dimensions: the universal and the local. *Universal church* means "the church of the whole earth." *Local church* means "the church of a given locality."

But since the Protestant Reformation we have a new type of church neither universal nor local. It's the denomination. The denominations have tried every type of government you can imagine, from rigid episcopal forms on the right to presbyterian forms in the middle to congregational forms on the left.

Still we don't have a solution. Why? Because you can't put Ford parts on a Chevrolet. You have to use Chevy parts. The denomination is not the same as the New Testament church of the locality, and so none of our guesses at New Testament structure will fit.

Once I went to Ecuador and saw the big, sweet bananas

they grow there. I said, "How nice. Could I take one of these plants home with me? Our bananas are always so small."

Someone said, "Well, it won't do much good, because it's too cold in Argentina to raise big bananas like these. You'd have to take our soil, our rain, our temperature—you'd have to move all of Ecuador to your country."

So it is with us. We've taken a trip to the primitive church and discovered the baptism in the Holy Spirit. And we've tried to transplant it to our church without bringing along the climate. We end up with short, stubby bananas. What happened? The Holy Spirit is still the same as He was in the first century. But it seems like He has been watered down—one gallon of Him to about a hundred gallons of cold water! We have weakened Him.

We simply cannot have effective biblical church government in a structure that is not biblical.

What is the biblical church? The church in the locality. The church in each area is one. There is no such thing as two or three or ten churches; the church is one, like God Himself.

When God revealed Himself to Moses at the burning bush, Moses wanted to know what His name was. God said, in essence, "Moses, you come from Egypt where there are many gods, and you need names to keep them all straight. But there is only one God. From me there are no others."

Moses didn't understand. He still wanted a name. And God said, "Listen, if we were many, we would need names. But I don't need one—I am who I am. I'm the only one."

"But when I get back to Egypt, I have to call You something. What shall I say?"

"Well, you'll just have to say that I Am sent you." What an odd name!

The same is true of the Church. People often ask me, "What church are you from?"

"I'm from the Church," I say.

"Which one?"

"The Church."

"Oh, come on, come on—you know what I mean. Which church are you from?"

There is only one church. In the New Testament they never had to think up a name for the church, because there was only one. When I was in Charlotte, North Carolina, I was told that there are 400 churches in that city. That's not really true. There is one church in Charlotte broken into 400 pieces. There can only be one church in each locality.

So we must find out how to put the pieces back together. We should go to the top of the highest building and say, "Lord, show me the church in this city as You see it." We are short-sighted. We think God is looking at just our congregation through a long tube from heaven, saying, "How nice everything is! What a nice organ they bought ... what nice carpeting they installed."

Listen—He's looking down and weeping. Through His tears He's saying what Jesus said as He wept over Jerusalem: "How often I wanted to gather your children together, the way a hen gathers her chicks under her wings, and you were unwilling. Behold, your house is being left to you desolate" (Matthew 23:37-38).

He sees the different pastors of the city as all co-pastors of His one church. If they are co-pastors, they should meet together, have fellowship, love one another. They should almost live together as the twelve pastors of the Jerusalem church did. They are the presbytery of the city, the elders in charge of God's flock.

In some places we are so wrong today that we call deacons "elders." So we have the strange arrangement of "elders" serving *under* pastors. We don't understand that the two are the same thing in the New Testament. Jesus is the Head who in John's vision in Revelation 1 was walking among the lampstands (the churches). Each church in each locality is different; it adapts to its local need the way the Jerusalem church developed one way and the Antioch church another. But all are under the lordship of Jesus

Christ. And through the leadership of the apostles and elders, the Kingdom of God must be brought to each place.

Is this a strange concept to us? A threat to our traditions? It is true that we cannot snap our fingers and instantly be done with denominations. Even our civil governments have come to expect them of us. But we must not let this keep us from discerning the true body of Christ in each locality. The holy Protestant tradition must not stand in the way of growth.

17

Beyond Sunday Morning

"Go therefore and make disciples . . . ."
—*Matthew 28:19*

Now it is time to write about the "mechanics" of making disciples. I hesitate to do it, because I am afraid you will run off and try to copy what I say without first being renewed by the Spirit. If you do, you will soon be frustrated.

The congregation must be renewed in its understanding of the lordship of Christ and the role of the slave—all that I shared in Part One—before it can use these mechanics. You don't need new wineskins until you have new wine. The most important thing is to get the new wine; then you can worry about the structure to contain it.

We didn't pick up these mechanics from a book or a

classroom. They came out of our *life* together. We began doing them without even thinking about it; we were simply trying to stretch to allow for the activity of the new wine.

First of all, discipleship has to start with pastors. If pastors do not get together as I explained in the last chapter and view themselves as the elders of God's one church in the city, they will never be able to make disciples of their people. Discipleship cannot spread from bottom to top; it must go from top to bottom. In order to make disciples, we must *be* disciples. Discipleship is not just a teaching, a classroom situation; it is a *life* situation. Pastors cannot take their old sermons and expect to make disciples with them. It won't work.

The will of God for today comes only in the group of ministers. As they wait before the Lord and pray together and love one another, God reveals His purpose for their city. God is finally able to speak to His shepherds as a group.

If we pastors are not submissive to each other, how can we expect the people to submit to us?

The other pastors of God's one church form an extremely important guarantee for the disciples that they will not be abused by a dictator. They know that their pastor is also a disciple, subject to the leadership of the city's presbytery.

It takes a while for a group of pastors to be formed as disciples. But it must happen. It's amazing what you learn. I was a proud Pentecostal who never dreamed that the Baptist, the Presbyterian, the Plymouth Brethren, or the Catholic brother could tell me anything new. I had the "full" gospel. But when we first got together back in 1967, I began to see how my congregation and I weren't so perfect after all.

Not every minister is a prophet or an evangelist. But together we enrich each other by sharing our ministries. There are now around twenty-five of us.

This group became one of the mother cells of Buenos Aires. Once it was functioning, we turned next to the selection of a few disciples for each elder. We had to guard against choosing people because we happened to like them, or because they were educated or rich—no, no. Disciples must be chosen purely by the guidance of God. In the natural, Paul would never have chosen Timothy. He was too young. He was also shy; Paul had to keep writing things like, "Do not be ashamed of the testimony of our Lord, or of me His prisoner" (2 Timothy 1:8). And on top of that, he had a chronic stomach problem. What a disciple!

But Timothy was God's choice.

Jesus prayed all night before He chose His twelve (Luke 6:12-13). The choosing of disciples is a serious, spiritual decision.

The cells began to multiply from there. The further we went, the more essential the lordship of Christ became—as you will see.

Each disciple has seven nights in the week, right? (We speak of nights in Argentina, because nearly everyone is working all day long.)

One night is given to the cell where the disciple *receives*.

On two nights, he *gives*. In one cell he is forming the lives of new converts; in the other he is forming the lives of future cell leaders. You see the multiplication factor which is functioning all the time.

So when a person becomes a believer, he goes only to one cell at first, a cell for babes in Christ. Soon he switches to a cell to train him for leadership. Then he begins to function as a full disciple—receiving from above and at the same time giving both to new converts and younger disciples. No one is drained by continual giving. But no one just sits and gets fat, either.

On a fourth night of the week (usually Sunday), we all meet together.

A fifth night is given to the family. This is a commandment. Single people must give the night to their parents. After all, family relations are very important in discipleship; this is a new way of life, not just a way of talk.

A sixth night is given to rest. This too is a commandment. We need it, because we seldom get to bed before one o'clock on cell nights. So we must rest for the sake of the Kingdom. The King needs us to be refreshed to do our job. That's why He gave Moses the Fourth Commandment.

Many Christians say their Sunday is a day of rest. How can they say that? It's the day they get more tired than ever. They get up early for Sunday school, then morning worship, then pass out tracts in the afternoon, then the youth service, then the evening service. We spread our four meetings throughout the week; they jam theirs all into one day! That's not a day of rest.

When God said, "You shall not do any work" (Exodus 20:10), that's what He meant. The clothing manufacturers put in labels that say, "Wash this garment like this, iron it like this," and so forth. When God made us, He said, "One day a week this machine has to rest." The doctors and psychiatrists wouldn't earn nearly as much money if people followed God's instructions.

That is why we stopped meeting on Sunday morning. We need to sleep! Everyone stays home and sleeps until ten or eleven o'clock on Sunday morning. It's different, but it works.

The seventh night is for reinforcement. Whatever element from the other six nights needs more attention gets it on the seventh night. The disciple goes to his leader to get special help on one of his weak areas. Or he goes to visit one of his own disciples. Or he reinforces his family relationships. Or he rests.

And once a month, all the cells go together to the country for a weekend—Friday night through Sunday noon. We share together, live together, confess our sins to one another, and build the community relationship among us.

Now you can see why our people must be totally committed to the Kingdom! All day while they are working, they are thinking about what they are going to do after work for the Kingdom. They are disciples twenty-four hours a day. (I don't think I have to worry about people copying us without being submitted to Jesus. They wouldn't last very long.)

What is a cell? *Cell* is the temporary name for a meeting of several people for certain purposes. It's not a Bible word. The proper name would be *church in the home*, but people get off the track when we use that. They think of going to a house and having a church service—a song, a Bible reading, a discussion, a prayer, and a dismissal. And that's not a cell at all. (Eventually we will come to say *church in the home*, once people have forgotten what the old thing called church was like.)

After about a year of using the term *cell*, we changed the name to *small community* in order to emphasize the sharing that is so important. We are working hard now to end the poverty in our congregation. After all, we are supposed to be the light of the world. How can we tackle social problems outside the church when we haven't solved them inside the church? Some pastors get very involved in politics to bring about the social justice—but they can't get it in their own congregation. We should start where our own word is heard and obeyed. Let us start with the people with the Bibles under their arms. They must carry out social justice before anyone else.

It's incredible to think that one brother in a congregation can have two TVs while another has no bed. It's incredible that one has two or more cars while another has to walk twenty blocks and wait for buses an hour every day. But it happens all the time in my country.

So we are emphasizing community in our church. When

we have stopped the poverty in our own congregation, then we will have the authority to tell the world about social justice. We are now cleaning our own house first.

A cell has from five to eight people. If it gets any larger than that, it starts to be a little church unto itself. We want the church to remain together with each person very conscious of his part in the Body. (Not every cell person belongs to our congregation. Some of them are Baptists, Nazarenes, or Catholics who happen to live on the same block and want to grow in discipleship.)

The leader of the cell has no title. Since God has begun to renew us, we have been very careful about titles. We haven't yet laid hands on anyone to name him a deacon, an elder, or whatever. Before, we used to do it all the time. I was the Reverend, an ordained minister. But now I realize that I couldn't even be a deacon in the primitive church—they had more spirituality, more wisdom, more power, more gifts, more of everything than the most highly ordained people today. My only title is Unworthy Slave.

Authority comes by spirituality, not by titles. Otherwise, you can be quite disappointed and wish you'd never set someone up as a deacon or an elder. If he grows spiritually, the disciples will submit to him without any title. But if he's not authorized by God, the title of Most Reverend won't mean a thing.

I don't say it's wrong to appoint leaders; I just say it's wise to wait and let God cause them to function. Then we can easily point them out.

The cells can meet anywhere at any time. If it's too hot in the apartment, they can go to the beach or the park, because there are only five or eight people. The hour of the day means nothing. It's not like a church, which in most places is unlocked only at nine o'clock Sunday morning and at seven o'clock Sunday night, and if you miss those times, you're out. (The way of the Lord is narrow, but not that narrow.)

The cell has two important things in mind: the groups

and the task. I used to be a task-minded pastor. I had goals I wanted to achieve, and I couldn't take time to think about the people I was using to reach my goals. I was like an executive in a business who sees each employee as nothing but a machine, a tool that is necessary to make a profit.

I had learned that attitude from the system in which I had grown up. As a young man, I was out preaching in the small towns. Whenever I went to the central offices of my denomination, I was hardly noticed. When I visited the Bible school, nobody said hello to me. I went to the rooms, visited the students, and that was all.

But after I became the pastor of a big church, it was different. Whenever I went to the central offices or the Bible school—"Oh, hello, Brother Ortiz, give me your coat . . . would you like a cup of tea?" I was now important to their task.

Pity the poor pastor who falls in disgrace! Suddenly he becomes a nobody once again.

But in the new life of discipleship, we love people regardless of their contribution. Each member of the cell is important. The leader realizes that each person has his own aspirations and hopes. The cell ministers to the need of each person.

So no one has to be begged to attend. There are no telephone calls saying, "Don't forget to come to the cell. Please come—please promise you'll be there." No, they come because they cannot help coming. They find themselves realized in the group. The cell meets their social needs, their spiritual needs, even their material needs; it lifts their burden and problems so that they are then ready to take on the burdens of the Kingdom.

But a cell cannot be exclusively group-minded. Otherwise it is nothing but a club of good people who go to picnics and parties together. The cell also has a *task*: the Great Commission of the Lord Jesus Christ. They must be making disciples, or else there is no reason to exist.

Yet the task will never be done if the group does not love one another. The two are tied to each other.

18

The Cell

*And he entered the synagogue and continued speaking
out boldly for three months, reasoning and persuading them
about the kingdom of God...*
*And this took place for two years, so that all who lived in
Asia heard the word of the Lord, both Jews and Greeks.*
—Acts 19:8-10

What is unique about a cell? How is it different from a home
prayer meeting? It has five elements: devotion, discussion,
programming, mobilization, and multiplication.

Of course, not all five are apparent every week. One meeting may be all devotion while the next is all discussion. But
all five must be included in the life of the cell. (We got them
from Acts 19, where Paul made disciples in Ephesus and they
filled whole province of Asia with the gospel. They worshiped the Lord, they had teaching, they planned how they

were going to reach out, they went to the various places, and they founded many new churches—some of them are mentioned in Revelation 2 and 3.)

I don't think I have to explain devotion. Prayer, worship, praising, confession, breaking before the Lord—these are all part of the cell's devotion life.

Discussion is the lesson of the Word of God.

But we do it differently than you think. We don't give a new lesson each week. One lesson usually lasts for two or even three months. Why? Because we don't go on to a new one until we are practicing the old one. Doesn't the Bible tell us to be doers, not just hearers?

Ours is a generation of hearers. The reason is obvious: We have so many speakers. If we speak and speak and speak, people have no time for anything beyond hearing.

Scientific studies tell us that people remember only twenty percent of what they hear—and lose even that after ten days if there is no reinforcement. So once we get outside the church building, we only remember twenty percent of the sermon—and we forget even that unless we practice it. Or unless another sermon comes along on the same subject.

What do you remember from your school days? You remember how to read and write, how to add, subtract, multiply, and divide, because you've continued to practice those things. But how much do you remember of the geography of China?

Jesus didn't say, "Teach them to observe all that I commanded you." He said, "Teach them to know all that I commanded you." That's why the discussion element of our cells includes practice.

The way we used to do it in our church was like this: We had a prayer meeting on Tuesday. We preached on prayer. "Pray, people, pray! Prayer changes things. Prayer is the most important thing." The people went home determined to pray more than ever before.

They came back on Thursday for the Bible study. We

were in the middle of Nehemiah, telling about the broken walls of Jerusalem and how Nehemiah rebuilt them. "What a man he was! We need more people like Nehemiah today." So the people forgot about prayer and thought about imitating Nehemiah.

Next came Sunday school. They were studying the Tabernacle with all its beautiful types of Christ in the courts, the Holy Place . . . ah, that's really important, too.

But then immediately they went to the morning worship where I preached on holiness. "Without holiness, we cannot please the Lord!" I told them. "God wants a holy people." So they went home thinking about holiness, forgetting all about prayer, Nehemiah, and the Tabernacle.

They were back on Sunday night to hear, "The Lord is coming soon! We must prepare for the Second Coming of Christ."

And so on for years and years. What could they do besides hear? Five messages a week, fifty-two weeks a year—260 messages! They would have been better off to say to themselves, *I'll listen to this one message, and then I won't come back to church until I'm putting it into practice in my life.*

So now we have only four or five messages a year. Since we began discipleship in 1971, we have had less than twenty lessons. But the church is completely changed. Why? We are practicing what we hear. That is the real point of the Word. The doctrine we need in our lives is not so much the articles of faith or the creed as it is the practice.

Listen to what Paul told Titus: "Speak the things which are fitting for sound doctrine." (Here comes the theology of the holy Trinity, right? No.) "Older men are to be temperate, dignified, sensible, sound in faith, in love, in perseverance. Older women likewise are to be reverent in their behavior, not malicious gossips, nor enslaved to much wine, teaching what is good, that they may encourage the young women to love their husbands, to love their children, to be sensible, pure, workers at home, kind, being subject to their own husbands, that the word of God may not be dishonored. Likewise urge the young men to be sensible .... Urge bond-slaves to be subject to their own masters in everything, to be well pleasing, not argumentative .... Remind them to be subject to rulers, to authorities, to be obedient, to be ready for every good deed" (Titus 2:1-6,9; 3:1).

What a sound doctrine! It doesn't have much to do with the Tribulation or the Millennium, but it's fantastic doctrine.

What is the creed? A statement of the philosophical definitions of our belief.

What is sound doctrine? An employee not being argumentative.

There are many good deacons in the churches who sign the articles of faith every year—they believe in the Virgin Birth and everything else—but aren't practicing sound doctrine. They still drive fifteen miles an hour over the speed limit; they have no intention of being "subject to rulers, to authorities" if it's not to their advantage.

Peter told husbands to "live with your wives in an understanding way, as with a weaker vessel, since she is a woman; and grant her honor as a fellow-heir of the grace of life" (1 Peter 3:7). Lots of pastors and deacons who have all their theology straight don't like that kind of sound doctrine.

"Wives, be submissive to your own husbands," Peter said in verse 1 of the same chapter. We have deaconesses who are just the opposite.

We discuss these kinds of things in the cells. Let's say the lesson is on husbands. The first week we discuss all the material of the lesson. The second week we review the material by questions and answers to make sure everyone understands what a husband is and how he should relate to his wife and children.

The third week we start over with the first point of the lesson: "The husband is the head of the home." We discuss how to put it into practice. The leader turns to Roberto and says, "Well, Roberto, are you really the head of your house?"

"Well, I tell you," Roberto says, "we've really been through a problem here lately. I guess I'm not the head of my home, because I don't know how to solve it."

"What happened?"

"Well, my father-in-law died recently, and he had a big dog that he really loved. We had to bring my mother-in-law to live with us, and of course she had to bring along the dog, since it's a remembrance of her husband.

"The trouble is, our apartment is too small for a dog. So we argue about it. I say the dog has to go. My wife says, 'Poor mom—she's so old. The dog reminds her of daddy. Please be kind and let him stay.' We're getting nowhere—I don't even know if I want to keep living there anymore."

Someone in the cell says, "Listen, Roberto—I can help you. I live on the outskirts of the city, and I have a big piece of land. Let me take care of the dog for a while."

But the leader says, "No, Roberto, perhaps God sent the dog to your home to teach you something. Listen, you are not the head of your home—but not for the reason you think. A head is not just someone who gives orders to everybody. A head is someone who brings solutions, who thinks out what needs to be done.

"How can a dog be worth all that trouble? He's tearing the whole family apart, and he's not even a person."

And someone else says, "Listen, maybe the dog shouldn't be in the apartment—maybe you're right. But maybe God wants you to learn to love that dog anyway. Come on Roberto—you're losing your wife, you're making the old woman unhappy. The problem really isn't the dog—it's you."

Roberto says, "Oh, no. I can't!"

"Don't worry," the leader says. "We're going to pray for you that God will give you the power to accept the dog. Come here and sit in the middle of the room." We all gather around and lay hands on him to pray. "God, give him victory over the dog. Make him love his wife and his mother-in-law. Please help him . . . ."

Roberto starts to weep. Finally he says, "Okay, I think I can do it now."

"All right," we say. "Now on your way home, stop in a store and buy the dog a new coat. If you don't have the money, we'll give you some. You must learn to love the dog. You are working out a solution to the problem in your home."

What Roberto doesn't know is that at that moment his wife is with my wife in another cell. She too is telling the story of the dog. And my wife is saying, "Listen, he is the head of your house, and you have to submit to him. Even your mother must submit to him now.

"If he says the dog goes, the dog goes. Why don't you see if you can find another place for the dog to stay, and you and your mother can still go see him once or twice a week?"

"I never thought of that," she says. "He really is the head, and we have to obey him. I'll talk with mom."

She goes home and convinces her mother to give the dog away. About that time, Roberto walks in with a new coat for the dog!

You cannot accomplish things like that in a Sunday morning service.

After we finish praying for Roberto that third week, we start in on Felipe, then the others. (You can see now why cell meetings take four to six hours.)

The next week we hear reports of what happened. Roberto says, "You won't believe what happened when I got home . . .!" We rejoice together.

The fifth week we move on to point 2: "Husbands must love their wives." Here comes the mystical part of marriage. We each take a rose or a box of candy to our wives, and the home becomes a heaven.

Eventually we get to the third point of the lesson: "Husbands must provide for their families." We all complain about the inflation. But then someone tells how he and his neighbors buy potatoes and meat in bulk, thereby saving money. Someone else shows how to budget better, to control the money we have.

You see, cells are not just for speaking about heaven and seraphs. We talk about the cost of living, about politics, about everything, because we are integrated persons. We are not just "souls." In the Kingdom of God, there is no such thing as spiritual gospel and a social gospel. It is all one gospel of the Kingdom.

And in all my illustrating, you can see how important submission is. If Roberto has a rebellious spirit, nothing works. Brokenness is not a matter of tears; it is a matter of obeying. I have seen people fill many handkerchiefs in a meeting and still not be broken. We don't need to weep so much as we need to obey.

Obedience and submission, of course, are present because of love and trust.

Finally, after two or three months, we finish the lesson on husbands. But all the homes are now revolutionized. We have become doers of the Word.

The cells are the real bone and muscle of the church. The Sunday meeting is only the skin. The internal cells must be strong and healthy, or else the skin will eventually die. But when the cells are alive and disciples are being made around the clock all over the city, the meetings are shining and brilliant with health.

Let us do what Jesus commanded. Let us turn the church right side up and begin the new life of discipleship.

19

The Promise of the Father:
A New Heart

"Behold, I am sending forth the promise of my Father upon you; but you are to stay in the city until you are clothed with power from on high."

—Luke 24:29

All that I've said so far is important to the renewal of the Church. But before renewal can really happen, I think we must know and understand the Promise of the Father.

So the purpose of these next two chapters is, first of all, to encourage and challenge you and to announce to you that the restoration of this promise is coming. The second purpose is to make us more humble in our relationships with one another as brothers and sisters.

When Jesus talked about the Promise of the Father, He didn't say, "Behold, I send *one* of the promises of My Father." (Some preachers say there are 6,000 promises; others say there are 3,000. I do not know.) But Jesus' disciples understood perfectly what He meant when He said, "I am sending *the* promise of My Father."

We can know and understand the Promise of the Father today because Scripture speaks clearly and definitely about it. But we have trouble with that, even though the Bible speaks of the Promise from Genesis to Malachi. If you had asked any Jew what it meant, he could have told you. But we have made so many problems and doctrines of Scripture that we don't know where one doctrine fits or where one begins and the other one ends. So to understand the Promise we have to go back to Adam and Eve.

Some say that if Adam and Eve had not fallen, we would be enjoying another type of life. Or some say, "Oh, if I had been as innocent as Adam was." He was innocent, but he failed. Innocence does not guarantee success. If Adam and Eve had not failed, Abel or Cain or others would have. Because man was made with a capacity for failure. When God made man, He knew man would fail. But He had a purpose in permitting failure—to glorify Himself with nothing.

Before Adam and Eve fell, God had told them they could not eat the fruit of a certain tree, but they did anyway. Man became conscious of good and evil and was then obliged to decide which he would do. But he was so weak he could not do the good and forsake the evil. His conscience condemned him continually for his failures.

"What can man do?" he cried. "How can I please God? I know the right way; I know the wrong way. I want to do the right thing, but I do the wrong thing. Oh God, this is not life! How can I meet Your requirements?"

Then God sent the Law of Moses; it was the written Word. It was plain and powerful with all its commandments and do's and don'ts. The people came to see if the stone had any consolation for them. They read the stone, but it always had the same requirements, the same commandments. They had the same failures, the same problems.

147

They really wanted to do God's requirements and to live in holiness, but they couldn't. It seemed that no matter what they did or how hard they tried, they could never maintain a life pleasing to God.

So God promised to do something to help His people. This Promise is in all of Scripture; the whole Bible is based on the Promise of the Father. In Jeremiah 31:31-34 He promises:

> "Behold, days are coming," declares the Lord, "when I will make a new covenant with the house of Israel, and with the house of Judah, not like the covenant which I made with their fathers in the day I took them by the hand to bring them out of the land of Egypt, My covenant which they broke, although I was a husband to them," declares the Lord.
>
> "But this is the covenant which I will make with the house of Israel after those days," declares the Lord, "I will put My law within them, on their heart I will write it; and I will again be their God, and they shall be My people.
>
> And they shall not teach again, each man his neighbor and each man his brother, saying, 'Know the Lord,' for they shall all know Me, from the least of them, to the greatest of them," declares the Lord, "for I will forgive their iniquity, and their sin I will remember no more."

God said this new covenant was going to be completely different from the covenant He made when He took His people out of the land of Egypt. It was not going to be a commandment from the outside, but *an urge from the inside*. He had said, "I will put my law within them, on their heart I will write it . . . ."

Usually the only part of the New Covenant which we preach and teach is the latter part: "I will forgive their iniquity and their sin I will remember no more."

But there is more to the New Covenant.

What is the difference between being "commanded from the outside" and being "urged from the inside"? Maybe this illustration will help you understand. When a mother tells her girls to do things in the house, they object; they don't want to be forced to do something. But when they bring their boyfriends home for the first time they are willing to do anything mother asks. Now there is an urge from within.

That is the way God wants us to serve Him—willingly.

But the Ten Commandments are a poor shadow of the will of God; they are just the topping. In the Sermon on the Mount, Jesus said, "You have heard that it was said, 'You shall love your neighbor and hate your enemy' " (Matthew 5:43).

But the will of God is much more than that.

Even the strict keeping of God's Law does not really exalt Him because He sees people serving Him under obligation, because they are compelled to. People who serve God because the letter of the Law compels them to serve Him are still under the Old Covenant. They have learned nothing about the New Covenant, and most Christians today are still living under the Old Covenant. They say, "I have *tried* to do this or that." They are saying they can't do what is right.

They live under condemnation. Even though they sing and praise and are God's people personally, they still have tremendous doubts and problems and fights. They do nice things in the church, but when you go to their homes, you know the problems they have.

They live under the Old Covenant.

Some people think the Old Covenant is the Old Testament and the New Covenant is the New Testament. This is wrong. The Old Covenant is the written law. The New Covenant is a new heart:

> "Moreover, I will give a new heart and put a new spirit within you; and I will remove the heart of stone from your flesh and give you a heart of flesh.
> "And I will put My Spirit within you, and cause you to walk in My statutes, and you will be careful to observe My ordinances."
>
> —Ezekiel 36:26-27

God did not say, "I am going to give you a new code of ethics, a new list of commandments." No, He said He would give us a new *heart*—a fashionable, modern unit with His will built into it.

This isn't something we do ourselves. Memorizing God's commandments doesn't mean we have them in our hearts. Under the Old Covenant, man learned God's commandments but still he couldn't obey them. Some people today still use the old heart, even though they have a new heart which they received when they were converted.

But with a new heart, with the built-in word of God, man can at last do God's requirements. But he can do them only by the grace of God. This is not a positional or theoretical grace; it is a practical grace. It is a dynamic relationship with God as *He* causes us to walk in His will by His Holy Spirit.

We must understand that the Old Covenant is based on written laws which have to be *obeyed;* the New Covenant is based on the giving of the Holy Spirit who has to be *followed.* If you can understand this, you will be the happiest person in the world, and you will live a new life.

The Holy Spirit is the whole will of God, not just part of it, as was the Old Covenant. Under the Old Covenant people were told: Don't steal, don't fornicate, don't lie. On the day of Pentecost, Peter didn't receive a scroll with new verses and different commandments on it. No. The disciples received the Spirit of the Promise of the Father, just as Jesus had promised.

Jesus had spoken about the Promise many times. In John 14:26 He said, "But the Helper, the Holy Spirit, whom the Father will send in My name, He will teach you all things, and bring to your remembrance all that I have said to you." When they received the Holy Spirit, their whole lives changed. They started to live lives beyond the requirements of the law. Tremendous!

They started to share things with one another. they started to love one another, to rejoice when they were persecuted. They had no Bibles, no Sunday school material, no tape recorders. They had only what the Spirit of God gave them—a built-in faith which caused them to walk in the ways of God. That's why they could sing in jail though they had been beaten and chained.

Let's see what a built-in new heart unit meant in the primitive church:

> You are a letter of Christ, cared for by us, written not with ink, but with the Spirit of the living God, not on tablets of stone, but on tablets of human hearts.
> And such confidence we have through Christ toward God, not that we are adequate of ourselves to consider anything as coming from ourselves, but our adequacy is from God, who also made us adequate as servants [ministers] of a new covenant, not of the letter, but of the Spirit; for the letter kills, but the Spirit gives life.
>
> —2 Corinthians 3:3-6

You and I are the letters of Christ to the world, too, written with the Holy Spirit. That is the Promise of the Father.

We can write letters of the Spirit only if we are ministers of the New Covenant. If we are ministers of the Old Covenant we can write them only on paper, not in our hearts. Any seminary or Bible school can make ministers of the letter, of the Old Covenant. But only God can make ministers of the Spirit in the New Covenant. The ministry of the Spirit is to give Spirit, not to say "Look at what the Law says, and do that."

Every Christian should ask himself, "What am I ministering? Letters that kill? Or the Spirit who gives life?"

I have to confess that for years I was killing people. I had the ministry of condemnation with the letter. Though I was very sincere and did the best I could, most of the ministry was just of the Old Covenant type.

If we minister the letter of the Law we kill, or condemn; if we minister the Spirit we give life to the people. We give them the ability to do God's will.

That is the challenge of the Promise of the Father which is the Holy Spirit in the New Covenant.

20

The Promise of the Father:
A New Power

The Kingdom of God does not consist in words, but in power.

—*I Corinthians 4:20*

It often seems that the person who knows the most verses of the Bible and the one who can best explain those verses is the most popular preacher, or the most spiritual layman. That is not the way it should be.

Now I am not speaking against the Bible; I am putting this precious Word in the place where it will shine brightest. If you put a candlestick under the table, no one will see it; if you put it in your eye, it will burn you. You have to put the candle in its place, in the candlestick in the middle of the table.

If we put the Bible under the bed, it is in the wrong place. If we put it over the Holy Spirit, it is in the wrong place. We

153

must put it where God wants to put it. This is the Book that guides us to real truth. The more I read the Scriptures the more I have thirst for the things the Scripture speaks about.

The Holy Book is a means, not an end in itself. I think that many of us have made an idol of the Scriptures. If the wise men had worshiped the star instead of Jesus, they would have created an idol. The star was just a help to lead them to Jesus; it was a shadow of the real thing.

There are some copies of the New Testament with "helps" in the front or back: "If you are sad, read Psalm 23"; "If you are in trouble, read Psalm 46." Ministers of the Old Covenant!

We give the shadow of the reality; Paul gave the Reality of whom the shadow speaks. We can be ministers of shadow or of real things. If we follow the shadow, we are going to get to the real thing. If we follow the teaching of the Bible, we are going to get to the real thing.

We must minister the Spirit. We must minister reality. If we give a verse *about* peace, we are ministering shadow. But if we *give* peace we are ministering the real thing. To give the reality is possible if we follow the Spirit.

Jesus said when He sent out the seventy, "Whatever house you enter, first say 'Peace be to this house.' And if a man of peace is there, your peace will rest upon him; but if not, it will return to you" (Luke 10:5-6). The disciples did not give verses on peace, but peace itself.

The New Covenant, instead of *talking* about love, puts love into action. The fruit of the Spirit—love, joy, peace, patience, gentleness, kindness, faithfulness, self-control, goodness—is much more than law. In fact, love is the fulfillment of the Law. If you have love, you have the rest of the fruit, too. The fruit of the Spirit is the fruit of the New Covenent.

If we only *talk* about peace or *talk* about love, if we only give some Scripture verses about these things, we are actually ministering the shadow of peace and love. But if we *give* peace and *give* love, we are giving the reality of those things.

That is the difference between the Old Covenant and the New Covenant. The letter is the shadow of reality; the Spirit *is* the reality.

The reality, under the Old Covenant, was behind the veil. Behind the veil was the Ark of the Covenant, and in it was Aaron's rod. Aaron's dried rod which blossomed and gave fruit represents the restoring of the authority of the New Covenant. It is the built-in law which I talked about earlier.

"Don't touch. Wet paint." That is the Law, but we can't resist touching it.

The Law says, "Do not leave litter," but we leave litter. The law is good, but it can't keep us from doing what we shouldn't do.

But the Holy Spirit makes us able to fulfill the law of the New Covenant:

> There is therefore now no condemnation for those who are in Christ Jesus.
> For the law of the Spirit of life in Jesus Christ has set you free from the law of sin and of death.
> For what the Law could not do, weak as it was through the flesh, God did: sending His own Son in the likeness of sinful flesh and as an offering for sin, He condemned sin in the flesh,
> in order that the requirement of the Law might be fulfilled in us, who do not walk according to the flesh, but after the Spirit.
> —Romans 8:1-4

This is the New Covenant.

It is up to you whether you want to keep on with the Old Covenant. But these are days when the Holy Spirit is in the business of restoring the authority of the New Covenant. The headship of Christ is being restored to the Church. He was always the Head, but we were not always attached to Him as Head. Praise is being restored. Worship is being restored. The gifts of the Spirit are being restored. But the greatest thing that is being restored is the Promise of the Father in its fullness: the New Covenant.

No heresy is preached by people who are guided by the Spirit. Heresies are formed by those who study the Scriptures and misuse them. Look at how many different doctrines there are, all claiming the Scripture—Mormons, Seventh-Day Adventists, Pentecostals, Presbyterians, Baptists. Almost every year we hear of a new doctrine that has started—all with the Scriptures.

But the Scripture itself is not dangerous. I believe in the use of the Scripture. So this teaching could seem dangerous to some people: the New Covenant is Spirit; the Old Covenant is the written letter.

We need to speak the word of Spirit and life, and not just repeat the written word. The fulfillment of the Word is through the Life He puts in us. Jesus said, "He who believes in Me, as the Scripture said, 'From his innermost being shall flow rivers of living water.' But this He spoke of the Spirit . . ." (John 7:38,39).

That is the Promise of the Father. From *inside* is the fountain of life—not in reading and in trying to fulfill the Scriptures.

It is one thing to be searching for a glass of water; it is another thing to have rivers of water inside.

The fullness of the Promise of the Father is so much more than the "little" Baptism of the Holy Spirit which we have inherited from our dear Pentecostal brethren (of whom I am one). In the first days of this century the Holy Spirit started to move again in the Church and the Pentecostals got together to make a statement of faith. They institutionalized an experience which was just beginning to be restored. They said something like this (referring to His Church): "We believe in the Baptism in the Holy Spirit according to Acts 2:4."

If you believe only in Acts 2:4, you are going to receive only Acts 2:4. And Acts 5:6,7,8,31,32,33? What about sharing selling, etc.? We don't pay much attention to these verses. That is the problem.

"Why," I asked myself, "have you for so many years stated, 'I believe in Acts 2:4' and not 'I believe in Genesis to Revelation'?"

So if you have that statement of faith, read Acts 2:4 and put: "I believe in the Baptism in the Holy Spirit according to the Scriptures from Genesis to Revelation." Acts 2:4 is just a very small part of what the Promise of the Father really is.

We cannot deny that God used the Pentecostal Church in this century. We cannot deny that it is the fastest growing denomination in all of Latin America. It brought to light something that had been hidden for years. The Pentecostal Church stresses the availability of the gifts of the Spirit today.

But the sorry thing is that when a person makes a denomination out of one doctrine, he loses the other doctrines. Because the truth is in Jesus and the whole Church, not in only one sector of the Church.

Jesus gives each leader of the Church a piece of the puzzle. If each one of us came with a piece of the puzzle, we could see the whole picture. But the person who receives an experience and makes a denomination out of that is going the wrong way.

The Catholic Church was wrong when it ousted Martin Luther. If they had heard him, the whole Catholic Church could have been renewed. How many sons, faithful to the Mother Church, have been cast out because they would not agree with it?

But we evangelicals are doing the same thing. We count only those with us who think as we do. But listen, if the

Pentecostal church had spread love as they have the speaking in tongues, the world would have written another history of this century. If the Pentecostal church, with the success it has had, especially in the Third World, would have put the stress they put in tongues into the fruit of the Spirit according to Galatians 5:22 and 23, the world would have been revolutionized.

We started with the Spirit but we finished with the letter, and quarreled among ourselves.

Then what is the "little" Baptism in the Holy Spirit in contrast to the Promise of the Father? We worship the Lord in tongues; that is good. But it is not yet the Promise of the Father.

The experience we have had is like getting into the river up to our ankles. Of course, people who live in the wilderness—dry, thirsty for water for years and years—feel that this is the fullness when they wade into the water.

But they stay there. When we say to our children, "Let's go to the river," we mean the riverside. But when God says, "Let's go to the river," He means into the *river*.

Sometimes an evangelist comes and makes splashes in that water. We get all wet and cry, "Revival! Revival!" But he goes, and we are again in water up to our ankles.

We have had many of those experiences.

We must get into the river until we do not feel the bottom, until we are taken by the river. The river of God takes us out because it goes where God goes. Today *we* are directing the Spirit in many ways. This is because we are still touching bottom—so we can go where we want to. But when we are floating, the river takes us where it wants us to go.

The river is the New Covenant.

In the Bible there is only one promise—the Promise of the Father, the Holy Spirit. All the other promises are tributaries to this. But praise the Lord, if we are faithful in the "little" Baptism in the Spirit, God is going to give us the full one.

994